# Z GRILLS

# WOOD PELLET GRILL AND SMOKER

# COOKBOOK

## THE SIMPLE GUIDE TO MASTER 200+ HEALTHY AND TASTY RECIPES FOR BEGINNERS

**HILDA FULLER**

# CONTENTS

# INTRODUCTION

## What Wood Pellet Grills Are

A wood pellet grill is basically a hybrid between a smoker, a traditional grill, and an oven. They can be used for many different types of cooking, even searing and baking. Wood pellets are used for fuel. Some wood pellets are meant to last a long time, while others focus on enhancing flavor.

Pellet grills do not cook food over a direct flame. Instead, they heat food indirectly by circulating the warmth through the grill, much like what an oven does.

## How the Z Grills Wood Pellet Grill Works

A pellet grill looks like a gas grill, with a metal hopper mounted to one side to house the wood pellets they burn as fuel. The resulting fire imparts a smoky taste because the wood pellets are made from flavorful hardwood species such as hickory, oak, pecan, and cherry.

Today's pellet grills feature an electronic thermostat with a digital display, so you can dial in a precise cooking temperature; the hopper automatically draws the appropriate amount of pellets into the firebox, where they're ignited. The grill holds the temperature steady, like an oven, adjusting the rate at which it burns pellets to maintain that set temperature.

## The Benefits You'll Gain from Your Z Grills Wood Pellet Grill

There are some key advantages to be enjoyed when using a pellet smoker. We've covered the most important below.

1.  A pellet smoker offers more options and versatility than a standard smoker. Depending on the model you choose, it will be possible to roast, smoke, barbecue, and even bake inside your pellet smoker.
2.  Pellet smoking offers the best results for smoked meat. This is because they are designed specifically to infuse maximum smoke flavor with indirect heat. When compared to smoking in a normal grill, the results are far better. For rich and complex flavor, a dedicated pellet smoker is an ideal choice.
3.  Flavor options are virtually unlimited. Pellet chips are made from natural wood pieces, with flavors like hickory, maple, apple, mesquite, cherry, and more.

4. Temperature management is simple because most pellet smokers have advanced designs with automatic timing and heat control. The hopper ensures a consistent level of smoke throughout cooking.

5. Most models reach smoking temperature within ten to fifteen minutes. Only gas grills are easier and faster to get to cooking temperature.

6. Pellet smokers are designed for serious home cooks, so they are generally large, offering plenty of cooking space. This means you can easily cook whole turkeys, chicken, duck and other game, large BBQ cuts, and anything else that you want to infuse with a rich flavor.

7. Unlike a charcoal or gas smoker, pellet models are easy to use. There's no need to measure or weigh the wood that you will use. Pellets are distributed as needed and cooking temperature is regulated by an electronic thermostat.

8. Value is incredible because a high-quality pellet smoker will last for many years without problems. Even though the initial price might be higher than a comparable gas or charcoal grill, longevity, ease of use, and amazing results add value.

# Using Tips for Your Z Grills Wood Pellet Grill

1. Take advantage of your pellet grill's searing capabilities.

Many pellet grills feature searing capabilities, meaning they can reach temperatures over 500 degrees. Again, check your owner's manual for information on your specific model.

2. Use lower temperatures to generate more smoke.

You'll generate more smoke at lower temperatures, particularly in the "low and slow" range between 225 and 275.

3. Use the reverse sear method.

Don't be afraid to smoke your meat at a lower temperature, then finish it at a higher temperature. This two-step approach is especially useful for smoking chicken with crisp (not rubbery) skin, or the "reverse sear method" often employed for thicker steaks or prime rib

4. Never allow the pellets in the pellet hopper to run out.

Never allow the pellets in the pellet hopper to run out. If this happens, consult your owner's manual before relighting the grill. If you must, set a timer to remind yourself to top off the pellets.

5. Experiment with pellet flavors.

Experiment with pellet flavors. Some brands of pellets are fairly subtle.

# Better to Clean Your Z Grills Wood Pellet Grill

It is often easiest to clean the inside of your grill at the same time as the outside because your grill will already be unplugged, cold and emptied of wood pellets. Cleaning the inside of your pellet smoker involves several steps to ensure proper pellet grill maintenance, including cleaning the grease drip tray, vacuuming and scraping the burn pot and scrubbing the grill grates.

## 1. GREASE DRIP TRAY

To clean the grease drip tray, first remove the grill grates and any extra cooking racks. Use a griddle scraper to scrub grease off of the surface of the tray and remove the scrubbed grease using a paper towel. Wipe the grease drip tray clean using a cloth or paper towel. If you want to clean your grease drip tray with soapy water or liquid cleaner, remove the tray from the BBQ first. Dry the tray completely before putting it back into your pellet smoker.

## 2. BURN POT

Regular pellet grill ash clean-out keeps your smoker operating in top condition. A clean smoker provides even cooking and produce the best tasting pulled pork, ribs, and grilled veggies — or anything else you want to cook.

To clean your burn pot, first remove the grease drip tray and heat deflector to access the burn pot. Pay attention to how they are installed so you can put them back in when you are done. The burn pot will often have a lot of ash build-up and debris that you will need to remove. The simplest way to clean your pellet smoker's burn pot is with a vacuum cleaner or ash vac. Use the hose to suck out all the ash and then wipe away any remaining ash or soot using a clean rag.

When deep cleaning your pellet grill after winter, you can take this a few steps further and scrub the interior walls of the smoker to remove any accumulated grease or dirt. After vacuuming the ash, use a scraper with a flat edge to dislodge scale from the sides of the smoker chamber. Scrub the loosened dirt with a non-metallic brush and wipe the fire pot with a clean cloth.

You can use a damp cloth to wipe the interior of the grill, but never put water directly into the burn pot. Use caution not to damage the electric elements and allow the grill to dry completely before use. Once your burn pot is clean, replace the heat deflector, drip tray, and grates.

If your grill is equipped with an ash container, now is a great time to empty it. Ash collection systems make it easy to remove ash build-up and allow you to clean your burn pot less often, as they collect much of the ash that normally builds up inside your pellet smoker.

## 3. GRILL GRATES

Cleaning your pellet smoker grates every time you use your grill keeps your food tasting delicious and fresh so your cookout guests are always satisfied. There are two ways to clean your grill grates; cold or hot. Follow these steps for how to clean your grill before or after use:

### Cold Method (Before Cooking):

Ensure your grill is unplugged and cool:

Remove grates from grill and clean with bbq degreaser or soap and water. Some pellet grills may have dishwasher safe grates. If not, they can be cleaned in a sink or with a pressure washer or garden hose. If they are painted, be careful with using a pressure washer.

Scrub the grates thoroughly: Use a brush or spatula to scrub the grates to remove any residue that remains.

### Hot Method (After Cooking):

Set your grill to the highest temperature: Grill grates are easiest to clean when they are hot — and your grill will do most of the work for you. After you cook, turn your grill to the highest temperature and allow it to heat up completely.

Do a burn off: Wait 10 to 15 minutes to let your grill burn away the remaining food and grease on the grill grates. Performing a burn off loosens any stuck-on grease and makes it easy to scrape off the ash.

Scrub the grates thoroughly: Use a brush or spatula to scrub the grates to remove any residue that remains. Because the grill will be hot, it is best to use a long-handled brush or scraper. You may also choose to clean your grill grates while wearing an oven mitt or grill glove to prevent burns.

# BAKING RECIPES

## Smoked, Salted Caramel Apple Pie

Servings: 4
Cooking Time: 60 Minutes

**Ingredients:**
- 1 Cup cream
- 1 Cup brown sugar
- 3/4 Cup Light Corn Syrup
- 6 Tablespoon butter
- 1 Teaspoon sea salt
- 1 Pastry for Double-Crust Pie
- 6 Granny Smith Apples, Cut Into Wedges

**Directions:**
1. Supply your smoker with wood pellets and follow the start-up procedure. Preheat the grill, with the lid closed, to 180° F.
2. Fill a large pan with ice and water. Pour the cream into a smaller, shallow pan. Place the pan with the cream in the ice bath and place them both on the Traeger to smoke for 15-20 minutes. Grill: 180 °F
3. To make the caramel, combine the sugar and corn syrup in a saucepan and cook over medium heat, stirring constantly until it coats the back of your spoon and starts to turn a copper color, then stir in butter, salt, and smoked cream.
4. To assemble the pie, gather the pie crust, salted caramel, and apples. Place one of the pie crusts into the pie plate and fill with apple slices. Pour caramel over the apples. Lay the top crust over the filling, then crimp the top and bottom crusts together.
5. Make slits in the top crust to release the steam and finish by brushing with egg or cream. Sprinkle with raw sugar and sea salt.
6. When ready to bake, set the Traeger to 375°F and preheat, lid closed for 15 minutes.
7. Place the pie on the grill and bake for 20 minutes. Grill: 375 °F
8. Reduce heat to 325°F and cook for 25 more minutes. When ready, the crust should be golden brown and the filling, bubbly. Grill: 325 °F
9. Remove the pie from the grill and let cool. Serve with vanilla ice cream. Enjoy!

## Tarte Tatin

Servings: 6
Cooking Time: 55 Minutes

**Ingredients:**
- 2 Cup all-purpose flour
- 1 Teaspoon salt
- 1 Cup butter
- 5 Tablespoon cold water
- 1/4 Cup unsalted butter
- 3/4 Cup granulated sugar
- 10 Granny Smith Apples, Cut Into Wedges

**Directions:**
1. Supply your smoker with wood pellets and follow the start-up procedure. Preheat the grill, with the lid closed, to 350° F.
2. For the crust: Place flour and salt in a food processer and pulse to mix. Add butter a little at a time while pulsing. Once it starts to looks like cornmeal, add the water until dough start to come together. Form a round with the dough, wrap in plastic and let it cool in the refrigerator.

3. While dough cools, place a pie dish or a 10-inch round cake pan on the grill; add butter and sugar to pie dish. Let it caramelize.

4. When the sugar caramelizes and has come to a dark amber color, take off grill. Arrange apple wedges in a fan formation covering the caramel.

5. Roll the pie crust into a circle big enough to cover the pan. Prick the pie dough with a fork and cover the pan with the pie dough. Trim the crust leaving room for shrinkage.

6. Place on the grill and bake for 55 minutes until apples are soft. Let sit for 3 minutes. While pan is still hot, place a plate over pie and flip over. Grill: 350 ˚F

7. Serve warm, topped with ice cream or whipped cream. Enjoy!

# Pound Cake

Servings: 8

Cooking Time: 60 Minutes

**Ingredients:**

➢ 1 1/2 Cup butter
➢ 8 Ounce cream cheese
➢ 3 Cup sugar
➢ 6 eggs
➢ 3 Teaspoon Bourbon Vanilla
➢ 1 Tablespoon lemon zest
➢ fresh strawberries
➢ whipped cream

**Directions:**

1. In a large bowl, cream the butter, cream cheese, and sugar. Add eggs one at a time, whipping in between. Add vanilla and lemon zest, whip.

2. Pour batter into greased loaf pans, about halfway full to allow cake to rise.

3. Supply your smoker with wood pellets and follow the start-up procedure. Preheat the grill, with the lid closed, to 325° F.

4. Place loaf pans on grill and cook for 1 hour - 1 hour and 15 minutes. Check the cake at 45 minutes, if golden brown, cover loosely with foil and continue to cook until a toothpick inserted comes out clean. Grill: 325 ˚F

5. Cool loaf in pan for 10 minutes before removing to a wire rack.

6. Cut into 1 inch slices and serve with fresh sliced strawberries, top with smoked whip cream.

# Focaccia

Servings: 6

Cooking Time: 40 Minutes

**Ingredients:**

➢ 1 Cup warm water (110°F to 115°F)
➢ 1/2 Ounce Yeast, active
➢ 1 Teaspoon sugar
➢ 2 1/2 Cup flour
➢ 1 Teaspoon salt
➢ 1/4 Cup extra-virgin olive oil
➢ 1 1/2 Teaspoon Italian herbs, dried
➢ 1/8 Teaspoon red pepper flakes
➢ As Needed coarse sea salt

**Directions:**

1. Measure the water in a glass-measuring cup. Stir in the yeast and sugar. Let rest for in a warm place. After 5 to 10 minutes, the mixture should be foamy, indicating the yeast is "alive." If it does not foam, discard it and start again.

2. Pour the water/yeast mixture in the bowl of a food processor. Add 1 cup of the flour as well as the salt and 1/4 cup of olive oil. Pulse several times to blend. Add the remaining flour, Italian herbs, and hot pepper flakes.

3. Process the dough until it's smooth and elastic and pulls away from the sides of the bowl, adding small amounts of flour or water through the feed tube if the dough is respectively too wet or too dry.

4. Let the dough rise in the covered food processor bowl in a warm place until doubled in bulk, about 1 hour5. Remove the dough from the food processor (it will deflate) and turn onto a lightly floured surface.

5. Oil two 8- to 9-inch round cake pans generously with olive oil. (Just pour a couple of glugs in and tilt the pan to spread the oil.) Divide the dough into two equal pieces, shape into disks, and put one in each prepared cake pan.

6. Oil the top of each disk with olive oil and dimple the dough with your fingertips. Sprinkle lightly with coarse salt, and if desired, additional dried Italian herbs.

7. Cover the focaccia dough with plastic wrap and let the dough rise in a warm place, about 45 minutes to an hour.

8. When ready to cook, start the smoker grill and set the temperature to 400F and preheat, lid closed, for 10 to 15 minutes.

9. Put the pans with the focaccia dough directly on the grill grate. Bake until the focaccia breads are light golden in color and baked through, 35 to 40 minutes, rotating the pans halfway through the baking time.

10. Let cool slightly before removing from the pans. Cut into wedges for serving.

## Chicken Pot Pie

Servings: 6
Cooking Time: 60 Minutes

**Ingredients:**

- ➢ 2 Chicken, Boneless/Skinless
- ➢ 1 Cream Of Chicken Soup, Can
- ➢ 1 Tsp Curry Powder
- ➢ 1/2 Cup Mayo
- ➢ 1 1/2 Cups Mixed Frozen Vegetables
- ➢ 1 Onion, Sliced
- ➢ 2 Frozen Pie Shell, Deep
- ➢ 1/2 Cup Sour Cream

**Directions:**

1. Supply your smoker with wood pellets and follow the start-up procedure. Preheat the grill, with the lid closed, to 425° F.

2. Cut the onion in half and place on the grates of the grill. If you"re using fresh chicken breasts, barbecue the chicken at the same time as the onions. The chicken is fully cooked when the internal temperature reached 170F. While the onion and chicken are cooking, prepare the pie crust by putting one crust in a pie plate. When the chicken and onions are done, shred chicken and chop onion into small pieces and place in the prepared pie plate along with the mixed vegetables.

3. Combine cream of chicken soup, mayo, sour cream, and curry powder in a bowl. Pour into the pie crust with the chicken and mix to combine. Wet the sides of the bottom crust with a small amount of water and top with the second pie crust. Push gently along the sides of the crust to seal the two pie crusts together.

4. Place in the and bake for 40 minutes, or until the crust is golden brown. Serve hot.

# Pretzel Rolls

Servings: 6

Cooking Time: 20 Minutes

## Ingredients:

- ➤ 2 3/4 Cup Bread Flour
- ➤ 1 Quick-Rising Yeast, envelope
- ➤ 1 Teaspoon salt
- ➤ 1 Teaspoon sugar
- ➤ 1/2 Teaspoon celery seed
- ➤ 1/2 Teaspoon Caraway Seeds
- ➤ 1 Cup hot water
- ➤ As Needed Cornmeal
- ➤ 8 Cup water
- ➤ 1/4 Cup baking soda
- ➤ 2 Tablespoon sugar
- ➤ 1 Whole Egg White
- ➤ Coarse salt

## Directions:

1. Combine bread flour, 1 envelope yeast, salt, 1 teaspoon sugar, caraway seeds and celery seeds in food processor or standing mixer with dough hook and blend.

2. With machine running, gradually pour hot water, adding enough water to form smooth elastic dough. Process 1 minute to knead. (You could also knead it by hand for a few minutes.)

3. Grease medium bowl. Add dough to bowl, turning to coat. Cover bowl with plastic wrap, then towel; let dough rise in warm draft-free area until doubled in volume, about 35 minutes.

4. Flour a large baking sheet. Punch dough down and knead on lightly floured surface until smooth. Divide into 8 pieces. Form each dough piece into a ball.

5. Place dough balls on prepared sheet, flattening each slightly. Using serrated knife, cut X in top center of each dough ball. Cover with towel and let dough balls rise until almost doubled in volume, about 20 minutes.

6. When ready to cook, start the smoker on Smoke with the lid open until a fire is established (4-5 minutes). Turn temperature to 375 F (190 C) and preheat, lid closed, for 10 to 15 minutes.

7. Grease another baking sheet and sprinkle with cornmeal. Bring water to boil in large saucepan. Add baking soda and sugar (water will foam up). Add 3 rolls (or however many will fit comfortably in the pot) and cook 30 seconds per side.

8. Using slotted spoon, transfer rolls to prepared sheet, arranging X side up. Repeat with remaining rolls. Brush rolls with egg white glaze. Sprinkle rolls generously with coarse salt.

9. Bake rolls until brown, about 20 to 25 minutes. Transfer to racks and cool 10 minutes. Serve rolls warm or at room temperature. Enjoy!

# Basil Margherita Pizza

Servings: 6

Cooking Time: 25 Minutes

## Ingredients:

- ➤ Basil, Chopped
- ➤ 2 Cups Flour, All-Purpose
- ➤ Mozzarella Cheese, Sliced Rounds
- ➤ 1 Cup Pizza Sauce
- ➤ 1 Teaspoon Salt
- ➤ 1 Teaspoon Sugar
- ➤ 1 Tomato, Sliced
- ➤ 1 Cup Water, Warm
- ➤ 1 Teaspoon Yeast, Instant

## Directions:

1. Combine the water, yeast, and sugar in a small bowl and let sit for about 5 minutes.

2. In a large bowl, stir together the flour and salt. Pour in the yeast mixture and mix until a soft dough forms. Knead for about 2 minutes. Place in an oiled bowl and cover with a cloth. Let the dough sit and rise for about 45 minutes or until the dough has doubled in size.

3. Roll out on a flat, floured surface (or on a pizza stone) until you''ve reached your desired shape and thickness.

4. Supply your smoker with wood pellets and follow the start-up procedure. Preheat the grill, with the lid closed, to 350° F.

5. On the rolled out dough, pour on the pizza sauce, cheese, and then tomatoes and basil. Place in your Grill and bake for about 25 minutes, or until the cheese is melted and slightly golden brown.

## Baked Irish Creme Cake

Servings: 4
Cooking Time: 60 Minutes

**Ingredients:**
- 1 Cup Pecans, pieces
- 1 Yellow Cake Mix, Boxed
- 1 Vanilla Pudding Mix, Instant Package (3.4oz)
- 4 Large eggs
- 1/2 Cup water
- 1/2 Cup vegetable oil
- 1 Cup Irish Cream Liquor
- 1/2 Cup butter
- 1 Cup sugar

**Directions:**
1. Grease and flour a 10" (25 cm) Bundt pan. Sprinkle pecans along the bottom.

2. In a large bowl, with a mixer, combine yellow cake mix, pudding mix, eggs, water, oil, and Irish Cream liquor. Pour batter over nuts in the pan.

3. Supply your smoker with wood pellets and follow the start-up procedure. Preheat the grill, with the lid closed, to 325° F.

4. Place Bundt pan on the Traeger and bake for 1 hour, or until a toothpick comes out clean. Remove from heat, cool for 10 minutes. Grill: 325 °F

5. While the cake is cooling, combine the butter, water and sugar and bring to a boil. Boil for 5 minutes, stirring constantly. Remove from heat and add Irish cream liquor.

6. Use a bamboo skewer to poke holes in the cooled cake. Spoon glaze over the cake. Allow cake to absorb the glaze. Enjoy!

## Baked Cheesy Parmesan Grits

Servings: 4
Cooking Time: 60 Minutes

**Ingredients:**
- 4 Cup chicken stock
- 3 Tablespoon butter
- 3/4 Teaspoon salt
- 1 Cup quick grits
- 1 Cup shredded cheddar cheese
- pepper
- 1/2 Cup Monterey Jack cheese, shredded
- 1/2 Cup whole milk
- 2 Large eggs

**Directions:**
1. Supply your smoker with wood pellets and follow the start-up procedure. Preheat the grill, with the lid closed, to 350° F.

2. Butter an 8" baking dish or a 10" cast iron pan.

3. Bring the chicken stock, butter, and salt to boil in medium saucepan. Gradually whisk in grits.

4. Reduce heat to medium and cook until mixture thickens slightly, stirring often about 8 minutes. Remove from heat.

5. Add cheeses and stir until melted. Season with pepper and salt to taste.

6. Whisk together milk and eggs in small bowl. Gradually whisk mixture into grits.

7. Pour the cheese grits into the buttered cast iron pan. Bake until grits feel firm to touch, about 1 hour. Grill: 350 °F

8. Remove from grill and let stand 10 minutes before serving. Enjoy!

# Smoked Blackberry Pie

Servings: 4-6
Cooking Time: 25 Minutes

**Ingredients:**

➢ Nonstick cooking spray or butter, for greasing
➢ 1 box (2 sheets) refrigerated piecrusts
➢ 8 tablespoons (1 stick) unsalted butter, melted, plus 8 tablespoons (1 stick) cut into pieces
➢ ½ cup all-purpose flour
➢ 2 cups sugar, divided
➢ 2 pints blackberries
➢ ½ cup milk
➢ Vanilla ice cream, for serving

**Directions:**

1. Supply your smoker with wood pellets and follow the  start-up procedure. Preheat, with the lid closed, to 375°F.

2. Coat a cast iron skillet with cooking spray.

3. Unroll 1 refrigerated piecrust and place in the bottom and up the side of the skillet. Using a fork, poke holes in the crust in several places.

4. Set the skillet on the grill grate, close the lid, and smoke for 5 minutes, or until lightly browned. Remove from the grill and set aside.

5. In a large bowl, combine the stick of melted butter with the flour and 1½ cups of sugar.

6. Add the blackberries to the flour-sugar mixture and toss until well coated.

7. Spread the berry mixture evenly in the skillet and sprinkle the milk on top. Scatter half of the cut pieces of butter randomly over the mixture.

8. Unroll the remaining piecrust and place it over the top of skillet or slice the dough into even strips and weave it into a lattice. Scatter the remaining pieces of butter along the top of the crust.

9. Sprinkle the remaining ½ cup of sugar on top of the crust and return the skillet to the smoker.

10. Close the lid and smoke for 15 to 20 minutes, or until bubbly and brown on top. It may be necessary to use some aluminum foil around the edges near the end of the cooking time to prevent the crust from burning.

11. Serve the pie hot with vanilla ice cream.

# Smoked Vanilla Apple Pie

Servings: 6
Cooking Time: 45 Minutes

**Ingredients:**

➢ 1 1/2 cups of self-raising flour
➢ 3/4 cup of sugar
➢ 0.3 lbs of butter melted
➢ 1 tsp of vanilla extract
➢ 1 egg
➢ 0.9-lb tin of pie apples
➢ sugar & cinnamon for dusting

**Directions:**

1. Supply your smoker with wood pellets and follow the start-up procedure. Preheat the grill, with the lid closed, to 350° F.

2. Combine the self-raising flour, sugar, melted butter, vanilla, and egg in a large bowl until a golden dough texture is formed.

3. Spread half the mixture in a pie dish and press the bottoms and up the sides of the dish.

4. Pour pie apple tin into the pie and spread out evenly.

5. Sprinkle the remaining mixture over the top of the apple evenly and place in the smoker.

6. Leave for 45 minutes or until the golden crust forms on the top.

7. Dust with cinnamon and a little sugar if desired.

8. Serve warm with custard, ice cream, or both.

# Savory Cheesecake With Bourbon Pecan Topping

Servings: 6
Cooking Time: 75 Minutes

## Ingredients:
- Crust
- 12 ounce Oreos
- 6 ounce melted butter
- Filling
- 24 ounces cream cheese - room temperature
- 1 cup granulated sugar
- 3 tbs cornstarch
- 2 large eggs
- 2/3 cup heavy cream
- 1 tbs vanilla
- 1 1/2 tbs bourbon
- Topping
- 3 large eggs beaten
- 1/3 cup granulated sugar

- 1/3 cup brown sugar
- 8 tbsp corn syrup dark corn syrup recommended
- 2 tbsp bourbon
- 1/2 tbsp vanilla
- 1/8 tbsp salt
- 3/4 cup rough chopped pecans (smoked pecans recommended)

## Directions:
1. Supply your smoker with wood pellets and follow the start-up procedure. Preheat the grill, with the lid closed, to 350 °F.

2. Wrap foil on the bottom and up the sides of a 9" spring-form pan (outside of pan).

3. Butter the bottom & insides of the pan.

4. Crust

5. Throw ingredients in a food processor until they are finely ground.

6. Spread in 9" cheesecake pan on bottom & about ½ way upsides.

7. Filling

8. Place 8 oz of cream cheese in mixer bowl with 1/3 of sugar & cornstarch. Mix until smooth andcreamy.

9. Add another 8 oz cream cheese andbeat until smooth, then add remaining cream cheese, beating until smooth.

10. Then mix in the rest of the sugar, bourbon & vanilla.

11. Add eggs one at a time beating well after each one.

12. Add the heavy cream and mix just until smooth. Reminder: Do not over mix.

13. Pour batter into the prepared crust.

14. Topping

15. Mix all together except pecans.

16. Sprinkle pecans on top of cheesecake batter.

17. Pour topping over cheesecake batter.

18. Place in a pan big enough to hold a spring-form pan. Pour boiling water in the roasting pan to come up about ½ way up the spring-form pan.

19. Bake at 350 °F for 75 minutes until the top just barely jiggles. Carefully take the pan out of water-bath and put on cooling rack.

20. Let cool for 2 hours in pan. After 2 hours put in fridge until totally chilled then serve.

## Smoked Cheesy Alfredo Sauce

Servings: 2
Cooking Time: 40 Minutes

### Ingredients:

➢ 1 Cup heavy cream
➢ 1 Stick butter
➢ 1 block Parmesan cheese
➢ 1 Sprig fresh sage
➢ 2 Pinch Nutmeg

### Directions:

1. Supply your smoker with wood pellets and follow the start-up procedure. Preheat the grill, with the lid closed, to 180° F.

2. Pour the cream into a saucepan along with the butter and place on the Traeger grill grate to smoke along with the parmesan cheese.

3. Smoke for 30 minutes to 1 hour, depending on how much smoke flavor you want. Turn the heat on the Traeger up to 300°F. Grill: 180 °F

4. Shred the parmesan cheese and add it and the sage sprig into the pan with the cream and butter.

5. Whisk until the cheese has all melted and season to taste with the salt and pepper and a pinch or two of the ground nutmeg.

6. While warm, pour this sauce on anything. Enjoy!

## Grilled Bourbon Pecan Pie

Servings: 6
Cooking Time: 45 Minutes

### Ingredients:

➢ 2 Tbsp Bourbon
➢ 1/2 Cup Brown Sugar
➢ 1/3 Cup Unsalted Butter, Melted
➢ 1/2 Cup Light, 1/2 Cup Dark Corn Syrup
➢ 3 Egg
➢ 1/4 Tsp Hickory Honey Smoked Salt
➢ Decoration Pecan
➢ 1 1/4 Cup Chopped Pecans, Coarsely Broken
➢ 1 Prepared Or Homemade Pie Shell, Deep
➢ 1/2 Cup Sugar
➢ 1 Tsp Vanilla Extract

### Directions:

1. Supply your smoker with wood pellets and follow the start-up procedure. Preheat the grill, with the lid closed, to 375° F. Meanwhile, prepare your pie crust in a 9 cast iron skillet or heat proof pie plate.

2. In a large bowl, beat the eggs until smooth. Add the brown sugar and white sugar and mix until smooth. Add the light corn syrup, dark corn syrup, vanilla, bourbon, melted butter, and Hickory Honey Salt. Mix until smooth. Stir in your chopped pecans and pour into the pie crust. Top with the whole pecans, if desired.

3. Grill covered for 35-45 minutes, until the pie is just set around the edges but still has a slight jiggle in the center.

4. Allow the pie to cool completely before slicing. Enjoy!

# Double Chocolate Chip Brownie Pie

Servings: 8-12
Cooking Time: 45 Minutes

**Ingredients:**

- 1/2 Cup Semisweet Chocolate Chips
- 1 Cup butter
- 1 Cup brown sugar
- 1 Cup sugar
- 4 Whole eggs
- 2 Teaspoon vanilla extract
- 2 Cup all-purpose flour
- 333/500 Cup Cocoa Powder, Unsweetened
- 1 Teaspoon baking soda
- 1 Teaspoon salt
- 1 Cup Semisweet Chocolate Chips
- 3/4 Cup White Chocolate Chips
- 3/4 Cup Nuts (optional)
- 1 Whole Hot Fudge Sauce, 8oz
- 2 Tablespoon Guinness Beer

**Directions:**

1. Coat the inside of a 10-inch (25 cm) pie plate with non-stick cooking spray.
2. When ready to cook, set the grill temperature to 350°F (180 C)and preheat, lid closed for 15 minutes.
3. Melt 1/2 cup (100 g) of the semi sweet chocolate chips in the microwave. Cream together butter, brown sugar and granulated sugar. Beat in the eggs, adding one at a time and mixing after each egg, and the vanilla. Add in the melted chocolate chips.
4. On a large piece of wax paper, sift together the cocoa powder, flour, baking soda and salt. Lift up the corners of the paper and pour slowly into the butter mixture.
5. Beat until the dry ingredients are just incorporated. Stir in the remaining semi sweet chocolate chips, white chocolate chips, and the nuts. Press the dough into the prepared pie pan.
6. Place the brownie pie on the grill and bake for 45-50 minutes or until the pie is set in the middle. Rotate the pan halfway through cooking. If the top or edges begin to brown, cover the top with a piece of aluminum foil.
7. In a microwave-safe measuring cup, heat the fudge sauce in the microwave. Stir in the Guinness.
8. Once the brownie pie is done, allow to sit for 20 minutes. Slice into wedges and top with the fudge sauce. Enjoy.

# Crescent Rolls

Servings: 8
Cooking Time: 12 Minutes

**Ingredients:**

- 1 Crescent Dough, Can

**Directions:**

1. Supply your smoker with wood pellets and follow the start-up procedure. Preheat the grill, with the lid closed, to 375° F.
2. Unroll the dough and separate into triangles. Roll up the triangles and place on an ungreased nonstick cookie sheet. Bake for 10 -12 minutes on your Grill. You will know that they are finished when the rolls are golden brown.

# Italian Herb & Parmesan Scones

Servings: 8
Cooking Time: 20 Minutes

**Ingredients:**

- 2 1/2 Cup all-purpose flour
- 2 Teaspoon baking powder

- ➢ 1 Teaspoon baking soda
- ➢ 1/2 Teaspoon garlic salt
- ➢ 1 Tablespoon Italian Seasoning
- ➢ 1 Cup Parmesan cheese, grated
- ➢ 2 Large eggs
- ➢ 1 1/2 Cup buttermilk
- ➢ 1/4 Cup olive oil

**Directions:**

1. In a large mixing bowl, combine flour, baking powder, baking powder, soda, garlic salt, Italian seasoning, and 1/2 cup of the cheese. Make a well in the center.

2. In a smaller bowl, whisk together eggs, buttermilk, and olive oil.

3. Pour into the well in the dry ingredients, and stir batter just until it's combined. It will appear lumpy.

4. Oil 12 muffin cups, spray with cooking spray, or line with disposable paper liners.

5. Divide the batter evenly between the cups. Sprinkle the tops of the muffins with the remaining Parmesan cheese.

6. Supply your smoker with wood pellets and follow the start-up procedure. Preheat the grill, with the lid closed, to 400° F.

7. Arrange the muffin tin directly on the grill grate and bake the muffins for 20 to 25 minutes, or until a toothpick inserted in the center of the muffin comes out clean.

8. Cool for several minutes before removing from the muffin tin. Serve warm with butter or olive oil. Enjoy!

# Donut Bread Pudding

Servings: 8

Cooking Time: 40 Minutes

**Ingredients:**

- ➢ 16 Cake Donuts
- ➢ 1/2 Cup Raisins, seedless
- ➢ 5 eggs
- ➢ 3/4 Cup sugar
- ➢ 2 Cup heavy cream
- ➢ 2 Teaspoon vanilla extract
- ➢ 1 Teaspoon ground cinnamon
- ➢ 3/4 Cup Butter, melted, cooled slightly
- ➢ Ice Cream

**Directions:**

1. Lightly butter a 9- by 13-inch baking pan. Layer the donuts in an even thickness in the pan. Distribute the raisins over the top, if using. Drizzle evenly with the butter.

2. Make the custard: In a medium bowl, whisk together the sugar, eggs, cream, vanilla, and cinnamon. Whisk in the butter. Pour over the donuts. Let sit for 10 to 15 minutes, periodically pushing the donuts down into the custard. Cover with foil.

3. Supply your smoker with wood pellets and follow the start-up procedure. Preheat the grill, with the lid closed, to 350° F.

4. Bake the bread pudding for 30 to 40 minutes, or until the custard is set. Remove the foil and continue to bake for 10 additional minutes to lightly brown the top. Grill: 350 °F

5. Let cool slightly before cutting into squares. Drizzle with melted ice cream, if desired. Enjoy!

# Baked Chocolate Coconut Brownies

Servings: 4

Cooking Time: 25 Minutes

**Ingredients:**

- ➢ 1/2 Cup gluten-free or all-purpose flour, such as Bob's Red Mill

- ➢ 1/4 Cup unsweetened alkalized cocoa powder
- ➢ 1/2 Teaspoon sea salt
- ➢ 4 Ounce semisweet chocolate, coarsely chopped
- ➢ 3/4 Cup unrefined coconut oil
- ➢ 1 Cup raw cane sugar
- ➢ 4 eggs
- ➢ 1 Teaspoon vanilla extract
- ➢ 4 Ounce semisweet chocolate chips, optional

**Directions:**

1. Supply your smoker with wood pellets and follow the start-up procedure. Preheat the grill, with the lid closed, to 350° F.

2. Grease a 9x9 inch baking pan and line with parchment paper.

3. Combine the flour, cocoa powder and salt in a medium bowl. Set aside.

4. In a double boiler or microwave, melt the chopped chocolate and coconut oil. Let cool slightly.

5. Add the sugar, eggs and vanilla. Whisking until well combined.

6. Whisk in the flour mixture and fold in the chocolate chips. Pour into the prepared pan.

7. Place on the grill and bake until a toothpick inserted in the center of the brownies comes out clean, about 20 to 25 minutes. This will yield a somewhat gooey brownie. Continue to bake for 5 to 10 minutes if you prefer a drier brownie. Grill: 350 °F

8. Let the brownies cool completely, then cut into squares. Store in an airtight container at room temperature for up to 3 days. Enjoy!

## Baked Cast Iron Berry Cobbler

Servings: 6
Cooking Time: 35 Minutes

**Ingredients:**

- ➢ 4 Cup Berries
- ➢ 12 Tablespoon sugar
- ➢ Cup orange juice
- ➢ 2/3 Cup Flour
- ➢ 3/4 Teaspoon baking powder
- ➢ 1 Pinch salt
- ➢ 1/2 Cup butter
- ➢ 1 Tablespoon Sugar, raw

**Directions:**

1. Supply your smoker with wood pellets and follow the start-up procedure. Preheat the grill, with the lid closed, to 350° F.

2. In a 10-inch (25-cm) cast iron or other baking pan, mix together the berries, 4 Tbsp sugar and the orange juice.

3. In a small bowl, mix together the flour, baking powder and salt. Set aside.

4. In a separate bowl, cream together the butter and granulated sugar. Add the egg and vanilla extract and mix to combine. Gradually fold in the flour mixture.

5. Spoon the batter on top of the berries and sprinkle raw sugar on top.

6. Bake the cobbler for approximately 35-45 minutes. Cool slightly and serve with whipped cream. Enjoy! Grill: 350 °F

## Ultimate Baked Garlic Bread

Servings: 4
Cooking Time: 20 Minutes

**Ingredients:**

- ➢ 1 baguette
- ➢ 1/2 Cup softened butter
- ➢ 1/2 Cup mayonnaise
- ➢ 4 Tablespoon chopped Italian parsley
- ➢ 6 Clove garlic, minced

- salt
- chile flakes
- 1 Cup mozzarella cheese
- 1/2 Cup Parmesan cheese

**Directions:**

1. Supply your smoker with wood pellets and follow the start-up procedure. Preheat the grill, with the lid closed, to 375° F.

2. Lay baguette on a cutting board and cut it in half lengthwise.

3. In a bowl, add butter, mayonnaise, parsley, garlic, salt and chile flakes. Mix well.

4. Spread butter mixture on baguette halves and top with mozzarella and Parmesan cheese.

5. Place baguette on the grill (if you like the bread crisp, do not use foil and if you like it soft, wrap with foil). Grill for approximately 15 to 25 minutes. Serve warm. Enjoy! Grill: 375 °F

# Vanilla Cheesecake Skillet Brownie

Servings: 2
Cooking Time: 30 Minutes

**Ingredients:**

- 1 Box Brownie Mix
- 1 Package Cream Cheese
- 2 Egg
- 1/2 Cup Oil
- 1 Can Pie Filling, Blueberry
- 1/2 Cup Sugar
- 1 Tsp Vanilla
- 1/4 Cup Water, Warm

**Directions:**

1. Combine all brownie ingredients and mix. In a separate bowl, combine cream cheese, sugar, egg and vanilla and mix until smooth. Grease skillets

and pour in brownie batter. Top with cheesecake and cherry pie filling, using a knife to blend to give it that marbled look.

2. Supply your smoker with wood pellets and follow the start-up procedure. Preheat the grill, with the lid closed, to 350°F and bake for about 30 minutes.

3. Let cool for about 10 minutes and enjoy!

# Baked Peach Cobbler Cupcakes

Servings: 8
Cooking Time: 30 Minutes

**Ingredients:**

- 2 Large Peaches, fresh
- 3/4 Cup sugar
- 2 Teaspoon lemon juice
- 1/2 Teaspoon ground cinnamon
- Yellow Cake Mix, Boxed
- 1 Can vanilla icing

**Directions:**

1. Bring a pot of water to a boil. Turn peaches upside down and cut a small shallow X across the bottom. Put peaches in boiling water and boil for 1 minute to help loosen the skin.

2. Drain the peaches into a colander and rinse off with cold water. Peel skin off peaches.

3. Filling: Dice peaches and place into a large pan. Cook peaches over medium heat. As it starts to sizzle, add sugar, lemon and cinnamon. Cook mixture on medium heat for 10-15 minutes until a majority of the juice from the peaches evaporates leaving a thick syrup.

4. Transfer to a bowl to cool.

5. Supply your smoker with wood pellets and follow the start-up procedure. Preheat the grill, with the lid closed, to 350° F.

6. Cupcakes: Follow the directions on box cake mix and put the mixture into cupcake pan with liners.

7. When grill has preheated, bake cupcakes for 13-16 minutes, until a light golden brown. Grill: 350 °F

8. When cupcakes have cooled, use a piping bag to pipe the peach cobbler mixture into the middle of the cupcake.

9. Ice with your favorite vanilla icing. Enjoy!

# Eyeball Cookies

Servings: 20
Cooking Time: 35 Minutes

**Ingredients:**
- 2 Packages Candy Eyeballs
- Green, Blue And Purple Food Coloring
- 1 Box Of Yellow Gluten Free Cake Mix
- 1/2 Cup (Optional) Granulated Sugar
- 2 Large Eggs
- 1/3 Cup Powdered Sugar
- 1 Teaspoon Pure Vanilla Extract
- 6 Tablespoon Melted Vegan Butter (Unsalted)

**Directions:**
1. Supply your smoker with wood pellets and follow the start-up procedure. Preheat the grill, with the lid closed, to 350° F.
2. Line two large baking sheets with parchment paper. In a large bowl, combine cake mix, melted butter, eggs (or egg substitute), powdered sugar, sugar (optional), and vanilla and stir until combined. (substitute 2 flax eggs for Vegan – 1 tbsp flax seed meal and 5 tbsp water per egg).
3. Divide dough between 3 bowls and dye each bowl a different color.(We used green, blue and purple).
4. Roll dough into tablespoon-sized balls.

5. Place about 2" apart on the baking sheet and grill until tops have cracked and the tops look set, 8 to 10 minutes. – Turn half way through baking, after 4-5 minutes.

6. Immediately, while the cookies are still warm, stick candy eyeballs all over the cookies.

7. Let cool completely before serving.

# Easy Smoked Cornbread

Servings: 4
Cooking Time: 75 Minutes

**Ingredients:**
- 2 cups self rising flour
- 1 1/2 cups white corn meal
- 2 cups sharp cheddar cheese
- 1/2 cup sour cream
- 1/2 cup sugar
- 1 Tbsp baking powder
- 1 teaspoon sea salt
- 1 12 oz can of evaporated milk
- 1/2 cup vegetable oil
- 2 large eggs beaten

**Directions:**
1. Mix all ingredients together well and fold into a greased baking pan (such as a round cake Pan).
2. Supply your smoker with wood pellets and follow the start-up procedure. Preheat the grill, with the lid closed, to 375° F. Smoke on 375 °F for 1 hour and 15 minutes or until toothpick comes clean and edges look brown.
3. Rub some butter on top and sprinkle a little Fred's Butt Rub on top before serving.
4. Enjoy!

# Baked Brie

Servings: 6
Cooking Time: 8 Minutes

**Ingredients:**

- 16 Ounce (16 oz) brie wheel
- 1/3 Cup honey
- 1/4 Cup pecans
- Crackers
- apple, sliced

**Directions:**

1. Supply your smoker with wood pellets and follow the start-up procedure. Preheat the grill, with the lid closed, to 350° F.
2. Line a rimmed baking sheet with a piece of parchment or aluminum foil. Using a sharp serrated knife, slice top—the white rind—off the brie. (Le the ave the rind on the sides and bottom intact.)
3. Put the brie, cut side up, on the prepared baking sheet and drizzle with the honey. Sprinkle nuts on top.
4. Bake the brie until it is soft and oozing, but not melting, 8 to 10 minutes. Let it cool for a couple of minutes and transfer to a serving plate. Grill: 350 °F
5. Serve with crackers and sliced apple wedges. Drizzle with more honey, if desired. Enjoy!

# Grilled Apple Pie

Servings: 4
Cooking Time: 40 Minutes

**Ingredients:**

- 5 Whole Apples
- 1/4 Cup sugar
- 1 Tablespoon cornstarch
- 1 Whole refrigerated pie crust
- 1/4 Cup Peach, preserves

**Directions:**

1. Supply your smoker with wood pellets and follow the start-up procedure. Preheat the grill, with the lid closed, to 375° F.In a medium bowl, mix the apples, sugar, and cornstarch; set aside.
2. Unroll pie crust. Place in ungreased pie pan. With the back of a spoon, spread preserves evenly on crust. Arrange the apple slices in an even layer in the pie pan. Slightly fold crust over filling.
3. Place a baking sheet upside down on the grill grate to make an elevated surface. Put the pan with pie on top so it is elevated off grill. (This will help prevent the bottom from overcooking.) Cook the pie for 30 to 40 minutes or until crust is golden brown, the filling is bubbly. Grill: 375 °F
4. Remove from grill; cool 10 minutes before serving. Enjoy! *Cook times will vary depending on set and ambient temperatures.

# Baked Pear Tarte Tatin

Servings: 6
Cooking Time: 45 Minutes

**Ingredients:**

- 2 1/2 Cup all-purpose flour
- 2 Tablespoon sugar
- butter chilled
- 8 Tablespoon cold water
- 1/4 Cup granulated sugar
- 1/4 Cup butter
- 8 Whole Bartlett Pear

**Directions:**

1. Supply your smoker with wood pellets and follow the start-up procedure. Preheat the grill, with the lid closed, to 350° F.
2. For the crust: Place flour and sugar in a food processor and pulse to mix. Add butter a little at a

time while pulsing. Once it starts to looks like cornmeal, add the water until dough start to come together.

3. Form a round with the dough, wrap in plastic and let it cool in the refrigerator.

4. While dough cools, make the caramel sauce. In a sauce pan, add 1/4 cup granulated sugar and 1/4 cup butter. Cook butter and sugar until it becomes a dark caramel, a couple minutes.

5. Pour caramel in the bottom of 10 inch deep cake pan. While the caramel is still hot, arrange pear wedges in a fan formation covering the caramel.

6. Roll the chilled pie dough into a circle big enough to cover the pan. Prick the pie dough with a fork and cover the pan with the pie dough. Trim the crust leaving room for shrinkage.

7. Place on the grill and bake for 45 minutes or until pears are soft. The pears will be soft and most of the juice will evaporate and thicken.

8. Let sit for 3 minutes. While pan is still hot, place a plate over pie and flip over. Slowly lift the plate.

9. Serve warm, topped with vanilla ice cream or whipped cream. Enjoy!

# Vanilla Chocolate Chip Cookies

Servings: 12
Cooking Time: 20 Minutes

**Ingredients:**
- 3/4 cup brown sugar
- 3/4 cup white sugar
- 1 stick butter, room temp
- 2 eggs
- 1 tsp vanilla
- 2 1/2 cups flour
- 1/2 tsp salt
- 1 tsp baking soda
- 1 cup Chocolate Chips

**Directions:**
1. Cream your butter and sugar together in a mixing bowl using a hand mixer or stand mixer on medium speed for about 4-5 minutes.

2. Once the butter is creamed, add the eggs and vanilla. Continue mixing for an additional minute.

3. Put flour, salt, and baking soda in a sifter. Sift it into your creamed butter mixture.

4. Scrape the sides of your mixing bowl with a rubber spatula, and then turn your mixer on to low speed.

5. Let it mix a little, and then scrape the sides again. Stop mixing when there are one or two streaks of flour left in the cookie dough.

6. Scrape the sides of your bowl and pour in a cup of chocolate chips, and turn the mixer to low again to mix the chocolate. It should take just a few turns for the chocolate pieces to be well incorporated.

7. Line a large baking sheet with parchment paper. Using a medium cookie scoop (about 1.5 tbsp), drop evenly spaced dollops of cookie dough onto the cookie sheet.

8. Supply your smoker with wood pellets and follow the start-up procedure. Preheat the grill, with the lid closed, to 350° F. Place the cookie sheet in your smoker, and let them cook for about 12 minutes.

9. Let them sit on a cooling rack while you continue to cook the additional cookies.

10. Cool for a few minutes to let cookies set.

11. Enjoy!

# Baked Pumpkin Pie

Servings: 6

Cooking Time: 50 Minutes

## Ingredients:

- 4 Ounce cream cheese
- 15 Ounce pumpkin puree
- 1/3 Cup Cream, whipping
- 1/2 Cup brown sugar
- 1 Teaspoon pumpkin pie spice
- 3 Large eggs
- 1 frozen pie crust, thawed

## Directions:

1. Supply your smoker with wood pellets and follow the start-up procedure. Preheat the grill, with the lid closed, to 325° F.

2. Mix cream cheese, puree, milk, sugar, and spice. One at a time, incorporate an egg to the mixture. Pour mixture into pie shell.

3. Bake for 50 minutes, edges should be golden and pie should be firm around edges with slight movement in middle. Let cool before whip cream is applied. Serve and enjoy! Grill: 325 °F

# SEAFOOD RECIPES

## Cider Hot-smoked Salmon

Servings: 4
Cooking Time: 60 Minutes

**Ingredients:**

- 1 1/2 Pound Wild Caught Salmon Fillet, skinned, pin bones removed
- 12 Ounce apple juice or cider
- 4 Pieces juniper berries
- 1 Pieces Star Anise, Broken
- 1 Pieces bay leaf, coarsely crumbled
- 1/2 Cup kosher salt
- 1/4 Cup brown sugar
- 2 Teaspoon Blackened Saskatchewan Rub
- 1 Teaspoon coarse ground black pepper, divided

**Directions:**

1. Rinse the salmon fillet under cold running water and check for pin bones by running a finger over the fleshy part of the fillet. If you feel a bone, remove it with kitchen tweezers or a needle-nose pliers.

2. In a sturdy resealable plastic bag, combine the cider, crushed juniper berries, star anise, and bay leaf. Add the salmon fillet and put the bag in a bowl or pan in the refrigerator. Let sit for at least 8 hours, or overnight.

3. Remove the salmon from the bag and discard the cider mixture. Dry the salmon well on paper towels. Make the cure: In a small mixing bowl, combine the kosher salt, brown sugar, and Traeger rub.

4. Pour half into a shallow plate, or baking dish. Put the salmon fillet, skin-side down, on top of the cure. Generously sprinkle the top with the remaining cure, cover with plastic wrap, and refrigerate for 1 to 1-1/2 hours. Any longer, and the fish will get too salty.

5. Remove the salmon from the cure and pat dry with paper towels. Sprinkle the black pepper on top of the fillet.

6. Supply your smoker with wood pellets and follow the start-up procedure. Preheat the grill, with the lid closed, to 200° F.

7. Lay the salmon skin-side down on the grill grate. Cook for 1 hour, or until the internal temperature in the thickest part of the fish reaches 150 or the fish flakes easily when pressed with a finger or fork. Grill: 200 °F Probe: 150 °F

8. Let cool slightly. Turn the fillet over and remove the skin; it should come off in one piece.

9. If not serving immediately, let the salmon cool completely, then wrap in plastic wrap and refrigerate for up to 2 days. Transfer to a platter and serve with some or all of the suggested accompaniments. Enjoy!

## Garlic Bacon Wrapped Shrimp

Servings: 4
Cooking Time: 11 Minutes

**Ingredients:**

- 8 Bacon, Strip
- 1/4 Cup Butter Style Shortening (Melted)
- 1 Clove Garlic, Minced
- 1 Tsp Lemon, Juice
- Pepper
- Salt
- 16 (Peeled And Veined) Shrimp, Jumbo

**Directions:**

1. Supply your smoker with wood pellets and follow the start-up procedure. Preheat the grill, with the lid closed, to 450° F.

2. Take one slice of bacon, and wrap it around each piece of shrimp, and lock it in place with a wooden toothpick.

3. Place the shortening into a mixing bowl and whisk in the garlic and lemon juice. Brush each shrimp with the sauce on both sides.

4. Place on the grill, and barbecue for 11 minutes.

5. Turn the grill off, remove the shrimp, serve and enjoy!

## Delicious Crab Legs

Servings: 4

Cooking Time: 30 Minutes

**Ingredients:**

➢ 3 Pound crab legs, thawed and halved

➢ 1 Cup butter, melted

➢ 2 Tablespoon fresh lemon juice

➢ 2 Clove garlic, minced

➢ 1 Tablespoon Fin & Feather Rub or Old Bay Seasoning, plus more to taste

➢ lemon wedges

➢ Italian Parsley, chopped

**Directions:**

1. If the crab legs are too long to fit in the roasting pan, break them down at the joints by twisting, or use a heavy knife or cleaver. Split the shells open lengthwise. Transfer to the roasting pan.

2. Combine the butter, lemon juice and garlic; whisk to mix. Pour mixture over the crab legs, turning the legs to coat. Sprinkle the Traeger Fin & Feather Rub or Old Bay Seasoning over the legs.

3. Supply your smoker with wood pellets and follow the start-up procedure. Preheat the grill, with the lid closed, to 350° F.

4. Cook the crab legs, basting once or twice with the butter sauce from the bottom of the pan, for 20 to 30 minutes (depending on the size of the crab legs) or until warmed through. Grill: 350 °F

5. Transfer the crab legs to a large platter and divide the sauce and accumulated juices between 4 dipping bowls. Enjoy!

## Spicy Shrimp Skewers

Servings: 4

Cooking Time: 6 Minutes

**Ingredients:**

➢ 2 Pound shrimp, peeled and deveined

➢ 6 Thai chiles

➢ 6 Clove garlic

➢ 2 Tablespoon Winemaker's Napa Valley Rub

➢ 1 1/2 Teaspoon sugar

➢ 1 1/2 Tablespoon white vinegar

➢ 3 Tablespoon olive oil

**Directions:**

1. If using bamboo skewers, place them in cold water to soak for 1 hour before grilling.

2. Place shrimp in a bowl and set aside. Combine all remaining ingredients in a blender and blend until a coarse-textured paste is reached. Note: if a milder flavor is preferred, feel free to adjust amount of chiles to taste.

3. Add chile-garlic mixture to the shrimp and place in fridge to marinate for at least 30 minutes.

4. Remove from fridge and thread shrimp onto bamboo or metal skewers.

5. Supply your smoker with wood pellets and follow the start-up procedure. Preheat the grill, with the lid closed, to 450° F.

6. Place shrimp on grill and cook for 2 to 3 minutes per side or until shrimp are pink and firm to touch. Enjoy! Grill: 450 °F

# Mexican Mahi Mahi With Baja Cabbage Slaw

Servings: 4
Cooking Time: 10 Minutes

**Ingredients:**

➢ 1½lb (680g) skinless mahi mahi, cod, or other firm white fish fillets
➢ coarse salt
➢ freshly ground black pepper
➢ chili powder
➢ lime wedges
➢ for the slaw
➢ 2 cups finely shredded green cabbage
➢ 2 cups finely shredded purple cabbage
➢ 4 tbsp reduced-fat mayo
➢ 2 tsp hot sauce, plus more
➢ 2 tsp freshly squeezed lime juice
➢ ½ tsp coarse salt
➢ for the marinade
➢ ¼ cup freshly squeezed orange juice
➢ ¼ cup freshly squeezed lime juice
➢ 2 tbsp extra virgin olive oil

**Directions:**

1. In a medium bowl, make the slaw by combining the ingredients. Stir well. Transfer to a serving bowl. Cover and refrigerate until ready to serve.
2. Place the fish fillets in a baking dish and pour the orange and lime juices and olive oil over them. Turn the fillets to coat thoroughly. Cover and refrigerate for 15 to 20 minutes.
3. Supply your smoker with wood pellets and follow the start-up procedure. Preheat the grill, with the lid closed, to 450° F.
4. Drain the fish and pat dry with paper towels. (Discard the marinade.) Season the fillets on both sides with salt and pepper and chili powder. Place the fillets on the grate and grill until golden brown, about 4 to 5 minutes per side, turning with a thin-bladed spatula.
5. Transfer the fish to a platter. Serve with the slaw and lime wedges.

# Grilled Salmon Gravlax

Servings: 4
Cooking Time: 10 Minutes

**Ingredients:**

➢ 1 center-cut salmon fillet, about 2lb (1kg), preferably wild caught, skin on
➢ ½ cup aquavit or vodka
➢ 4 whole juniper berries
➢ ¼ cup finely chopped fresh dill, plus more
➢ lemon wedges
➢ for the rub
➢ 3 tbsp granulated light brown sugar or low-carb substitute
➢ 2 tbsp coarse salt
➢ 2 tsp freshly ground black pepper
➢ 1 tsp freshly ground white pepper
➢ 1 tsp ground coriander

**Directions:**

1. Run your fingers over the fillet, feeling for bones. Remove them with kitchen tweezers or needle-nosed pliers. Rinse the salmon under cold running water and pat dry with paper towels.
2. Place the salmon skin side down in a nonreactive baking dish and pour the aquavit over it. Crush the berries with the flat of a chef's knife and add them to the dish. Cover and refrigerate for 1 hour.
3. In a small bowl, make the rub by combining the ingredients.

4. Remove the salmon from the aquavit and pat dry with paper towels. Discard the soaking liquid and juniper berries. Rinse out the baking dish and place the salmon in the dish. Lightly but evenly sprinkle the rub on the flesh side of the fillet and gently distribute it with your fingertips. Scatter the dill over the top. Cover the dish and refrigerate for 4 hours.

5. Supply your smoker with wood pellets and follow the start-up procedure. Preheat the grill, with the lid closed, to 400° F.

6. With a sharp knife, slice the fillet into 4 equal portions. Place the fillets on the grate and grill until the fish is somewhat opaque but still translucent in the center and the internal temperature reaches 125°F (52°C), about 3 to 5 minutes per side.

7. Transfer the fillets to a platter. Scatter more dill over the top. Serve with lemon wedges.

# Smoked Sugar Halibut

Servings: 8
Cooking Time: 120 Minutes

**Ingredients:**

➢ 1/4 cup granulated sugar
➢ 1/4 cup brown sugar
➢ 1/2 cup kosher salt
➢ 1 tsp ground coriander
➢ 2 lbs fresh halibut

**Directions:**

1. In a small bowl, mix the sugars, salt,and coriander together. Season the halibut on all sides.

2. Wrap the halibut in plastic wrap, place on a rimmed sheet pan,and brine in the fridge for 3 hours.

3. Remove the plastic wrap and rinse the fish. Pat it dry. Set it on a drying rack over a sheet pan for 1-2 hours in the fridge.

4. Supply your smoker with wood pellets and follow the start-up procedure. Preheat the grill, with the lid closed, to 200° F. Smoke the fish for 2 hours or until its internal temperature reaches 140 °F.

5. Serve your preferred sauce with the fish.

# Smoked Cedar Plank Salmon

Servings: 4
Cooking Time: 20 Minutes

**Ingredients:**

➢ 1/4 Cup Brown Sugar
➢ 1/2 Tablespoon Olive Oil
➢ Competition Smoked Seasoning
➢ 4 Salmon Fillets, Skin Off

**Directions:**

1. Soak the untreated cedar plank in water for 24 hours before grilling. When ready to grill, remove and wipe down.

2. Supply your smoker with wood pellets and follow the start-up procedure. Preheat the grill, with the lid closed, to 350° F.

3. In a small bowl, mix the brown sugar, oil, and Lemon Pepper, Garlic, and Herb seasoning. Rub generously over the salmon fillets.

4. Place the plank over indirect heat, then lay the salmon on the plank and grill for 15-20 minutes, or until the salmon is cooked through and flakes easily with a fork. Remove from the heat and serve immediately.

# Simple Glazed Salmon Fillets

Servings: 2
Cooking Time: 25 Minutes

**Ingredients:**
- 4 (6-8 oz) center-cut salmon fillets, skin on
- Fin & Feather Rub
- 1/2 Cup mayonnaise
- 2 Tablespoon Dijon mustard
- 1 Tablespoon fresh lemon juice
- 1 Tablespoon fresh chopped tarragon or dill
- lemon wedges

**Directions:**
1. Season the fillets with the Traeger Fin & Feather Rub.
2. Make the Glaze: Combine the mayonnaise and mustard in a small bowl. Stir in the lemon juice and dill or tarragon.
3. Spread the flesh-side of the fillets with the glaze.
4. Supply your smoker with wood pellets and follow the start-up procedure. Preheat the grill, with the lid closed, to 350° F.
5. Arrange the salmon fillets on the grill grate, skin-side down. Grill for 25 to 30 minutes, or until the salmon is opaque and flakes easily with a fork. Grill: 350 °F
6. Transfer to a platter or plates, garnish with sliced lemons and chopped dill and serve immediately. Enjoy!

# Grilled Trout With Citrus & Basil

Servings: 4
Cooking Time: 10 Minutes

**Ingredients:**
- 6 Whole Trout
- 2 Teaspoon Blackened Saskatchewan Rub
- 10 Sprig fresh basil
- 2 Lemons, cut in half
- extra-virgin olive oil

**Directions:**
1. Supply your smoker with wood pellets and follow the start-up procedure. Preheat the grill, with the lid closed, to 450° F.
2. Season the center cavity of the trout with the Traeger Blackened Saskatchewan. Place two sprigs of Basil in each cavity, then add 4 lemon halves.
3. Next tie the fish closed using the Butchers twine, and then rub with olive oil.
4. Place the trout on the hot grill and cook 5 minutes on each side. Enjoy! Grill: 450 °F

# Delicious Jerk Shrimp

Servings: 8
Cooking Time: 10 Minutes

**Ingredients:**
- 1 Tablespoon brown sugar
- 1 Tablespoon smoked paprika
- 1 Teaspoon garlic powder
- 1/4 Teaspoon Thyme, ground
- 1/4 Teaspoon ground cayenne pepper
- 1 Teaspoon sea salt
- 1 lime zest
- 2 Pound shrimp in shell
- 3 Tablespoon olive oil

**Directions:**
1. Combine spices, salt, and lime zest in a small bowl and mix. Place shrimp into a large bowl, then drizzle in the olive oil, Add the spice mixture and toss to combine, making sure every shrimp is kissed with deliciousness.

2. Supply your smoker with wood pellets and follow the start-up procedure. Preheat the grill, with the lid closed, to 450° F.

3. Arrange the shrimp on the grill and cook for 2 – 3 minutes per side, until firm, opaque, and cooked through. Grill: 450 °F

4. Serve with lime wedges, fresh cilantro, mint, and Caribbean Hot Pepper Sauce. Enjoy!

# Smoked Salmon Candy

Servings: 4

Cooking Time: 180 Minutes

**Ingredients:**

➢ 2 Cup gin
➢ 1 Cup dark brown sugar
➢ 1/2 Cup kosher salt
➢ 1 Cup maple syrup
➢ 1 Tablespoon black pepper
➢ 3 Pound salmon
➢ vegetable oil
➢ dark brown sugar

**Directions:**

1. In a large bowl, combine all ingredients for the cure.

2. Cut the salmon into 2 ounce pieces and place in the cure.

3. Cover and refrigerate overnight.

4. Supply your smoker with wood pellets and follow the start-up procedure. Preheat the grill, with the lid closed, to 180° F.

5. Spray foil with vegetable oil. Place salmon on foil and sprinkle with additional brown sugar.

6. Place foil directly on the grill grate. Close the lid and smoke the salmon for 3 to 4 hours or until fully cooked. Grill: 180 °F

7. Serve hot or chilled. Enjoy!

# Lime Mahi Mahi Fillets

Servings: 4

Cooking Time: 8 Minutes

**Ingredients:**

➢ 3/4 cup extra-virgin olive oil
➢ 1 clove garlic, minced
➢ 1/8 teaspoon ground black pepper
➢ 1/2 teaspoon cayenne pepper
➢ 2 tablespoons dill weed.
➢ 1 pinch salt
➢ 2 tablespoons lime juice
➢ 1/8 teaspoon grated lime peel
➢ 2 (4 ounce) mahi mahi fillets

**Directions:**

1. Supply your smoker with wood pellets and follow the start-up procedure. Preheat the grill, with the lid closed, to 325° F.

2. Lightly oil the grate.

3. Combine in a bowl the extra-virgin olive oil, minced garlic, black pepper, cayenne pepper, salt, lime juice, and grated lime zest.

4. Wisk to prepare the marinade.

5. Place the mahi mahi fillets in the marinade and turn to coat.

6. Allow to marinate at least 15 minutes.

7. Cook on preheated grill until fish flakes easily with a fork and is lightly browned ( Typically 3 to 4 minutes per side).

8. Garnish with the twists of lime zest to serve.

# Dijon-smoked Halibut

Servings: 6

Cooking Time: 120 Minutes

**Ingredients:**

➢ 4 (6-ounce) halibut steaks
➢ ¼ cup extra-virgin olive oil

- ➤ 2 teaspoons kosher salt
- ➤ 1 teaspoon freshly ground black pepper
- ➤ ½ cup mayonnaise
- ➤ ½ cup sweet pickle relish
- ➤ ¼ cup finely chopped sweet onion
- ➤ ¼ cup chopped roasted red pepper
- ➤ ¼ cup finely chopped tomato
- ➤ ¼ cup finely chopped cucumber
- ➤ 2 tablespoons Dijon mustard
- ➤ 1 teaspoon minced garlic

**Directions:**

1. Rub the halibut steaks with the olive oil and season on both sides with the salt and pepper. Transfer to a plate, cover with plastic wrap, and refrigerate for 4 hours.

2. Supply your smoker with wood pellets and follow the start-up procedure. Preheat, with the lid closed, to 200°F.

3. Remove the halibut from the refrigerator and rub with the mayonnaise.

4. Put the fish directly on the grill grate, close the lid, and smoke for 2 hours, or until opaque and an instant-read thermometer inserted in the fish reads 140°F.

5. While the fish is smoking, combine the pickle relish, onion, roasted red pepper, tomato, cucumber, Dijon mustard, and garlic in a medium bowl. Refrigerate the mustard relish until ready to serve.

6. Serve the halibut steaks hot with the mustard relish.

# Teriyaki Smoked Honey Tilapia

Servings: 4
Cooking Time: 120 Minutes

**Ingredients:**

- ➤ 4 tilapia fillets
- ➤ 1 cup teriyaki sauce
- ➤ 2/3 cup honey
- ➤ 1 tbsp sriracha sauce
- ➤ Green onions (optional)

**Directions:**

1. In a large bowl, make the marinade by mixing together the teriyaki sauce, honey, and sriracha. Make sure honey is dissolved and well blended.

2. Place the tilapia fillets in the marinade. Turn the fillets so they are completely coated. Cover with a plastic wrap and marinate in the fridge for about 2 hours.

3. Supply your smoker with wood pellets and follow the start-up procedure. Preheat the grill, with the lid closed, to 275° F.

4. Remove the tilapia fillets from the marinade and transfer them to the grill. Smoke the fillets until they reach an internal temperature of 145°F, about 2 hours.

5. Sprinkle with green onions if desired.

# Smoked Trout

Servings: 6
Cooking Time: 120 Minutes

**Ingredients:**

- ➤ 8 rainbow trout fillets
- ➤ 1 Gallon water
- ➤ 1/4 Cup salt
- ➤ 1/2 Cup brown sugar
- ➤ 1 Tablespoon black pepper
- ➤ 2 Tablespoon soy sauce

**Directions:**

1. Clean the fresh fish and butterfly them.

2. For the Brine: Combine one gallon water, brown sugar, soy sauce, salt and pepper and stir until salt and sugar are dissolved. Brine the trout in the refrigerator for 60 minutes.

3. Supply your smoker with wood pellets and follow the start-up procedure. Preheat the grill, with the lid closed, to 225° F.

4. Remove the fish from the brine and pat dry. Place fish directly on grill grate for 1-1/2 to 2 hours, depending on the thickness of the trout. Fish is done when it turns opaque and starts to flake. Serve hot or cold. Enjoy! Grill: 225 °F

5. Fish is done when it turns opaque and starts to flake. Serve hot or cold. Enjoy!

# Charleston Crab Cakes With Remoulade

Servings: 4
Cooking Time: 45 Minutes

**Ingredients:**

- 1¼ cups mayonnaise
- ¼ cup yellow mustard
- 2 tablespoons sweet pickle relish, with its juices
- 1 tablespoon smoked paprika
- 2 teaspoons Cajun seasoning
- 2 teaspoons prepared horseradish
- 1 teaspoon hot sauce
- 1 garlic clove, finely minced
- 2 pounds fresh lump crabmeat, picked clean
- 20 butter crackers (such as Ritz brand), crushed
- 2 tablespoons Dijon mustard
- 1 cup mayonnaise
- 2 tablespoons freshly squeezed lemon juice
- 1 tablespoon salted butter, melted
- 1 tablespoon Worcestershire sauce
- 1 tablespoon Old Bay seasoning
- 2 teaspoons chopped fresh parsley
- 1 teaspoon ground mustard
- 2 eggs, beaten

- ¼ cup extra-virgin olive oil, divided

**Directions:**

1. For the remoulade:

2. In a small bowl, combine the mayonnaise, mustard, pickle relish, paprika, Cajun seasoning, horseradish, hot sauce, and garlic.

3. Refrigerate until ready to serve.

4. For the crab cakes:

5. Supply your smoker with wood pellets and follow the start-up procedure. Preheat, with the lid closed, to 375°F.

6. Spread the crabmeat on a foil-lined baking sheet and place over indirect heat on the grill, with the lid closed, for 30 minutes.

7. Remove from the heat and let cool for 15 minutes.

8. While the crab cools, combine the crushed crackers, Dijon mustard, mayonnaise, lemon juice, melted butter, Worcestershire sauce, Old Bay, parsley, ground mustard, and eggs until well incorporated.

9. Fold in the smoked crabmeat, then shape the mixture into 8 (1-inch-thick) crab cakes.

10. In a large skillet or cast-iron pan on the grill, heat 2 tablespoons of olive oil. Add half of the crab cakes, close the lid, and smoke for 4 to 5 minutes on each side, or until crispy and golden brown.

11. Remove the crab cakes from the pan and transfer to a wire rack to drain. Pat them to remove any excess oil.

12. Repeat steps 6 and 7 with the remaining oil and crab cakes.

13. Serve the crab cakes with the remoulade.

# Sweet Mandarin Salmon

Servings: 2
Cooking Time: 10 Minutes

**Ingredients:**

➤ 1 Whole lime juice
➤ 1 Teaspoon sesame oil
➤ 1 1/2 Cup Mandarin Orange Sauce
➤ 1 1/2 Tablespoon soy sauce
➤ 2 Tablespoon cilantro, finely chopped
➤ Freshly cracked black pepper
➤ 1 Whole (4 oz) wild salmon fillets

**Directions:**

1. Supply your smoker with wood pellets and follow the start-up procedure. Preheat the grill, with the lid closed, to 375° F.
2. For the glaze, combine Mandarin orange sauce, lime juice, sesame oil, soy sauce, cilantro and fresh cracked black pepper. Mix together.
3. Cut the salmon into 4 fillets. Brush with glaze and place directly on the grill grate, skin side down.
4. Cook until salmon reaches an internal temperature of 155 degrees F (about 15-20 minutes). Half way through cook time, brush salmon again with the glaze.
5. Remove the salmon from the grill and serve with remaining glaze if desired. Enjoy!

# Grilled Lemon Lobster Tails

Servings: 3
Cooking Time: 7 Minutes

**Ingredients:**

➤ 6 lobster tails
➤ 1/4 cup melted butter
➤ 1/4 cup fresh lemon juice
➤ 1 tablespoon fresh dill
➤ 1 teaspoon salt
➤ 6 lime wedges

**Directions:**

1. Supply your smoker with wood pellets and follow the start-up procedure. Preheat the grill, with the lid closed, to 375° F.
2. Split the lobster tails in half place then back side down.
3. Cut down through the center to the shell the whole length of each tail.
4. Pull the shell back, exposing the meat.
5. Pat the lobster tails with paper towel to dry.
6. Combine in a small mixing bowl the butter, lemon juice, dill, and salt until the salt has dissolved.
7. Brush the mixture onto the flesh side of each lobster tail.
8. Place the lobster tails onto the grill and cook for 5 to 7 minutes, turning them once during the cooking process. (The shells should turn a bright pink).
9. Remove the heat.
10. Serve with lime wedges!

# Garlic Pepper Shrimp Pesto Bruschetta

Servings: 12
Cooking Time: 15 Minutes

**Ingredients:**

➤ 12 Slices Bread, Baguette
➤ 1/2 Tsp Chili Pepper Flakes
➤ 1/2 Tsp Garlic Powder
➤ 4 Cloves Garlic, Minced
➤ 2 Tbsp Olive Oil
➤ 1/2 Tsp Paprika, Smoked
➤ 1/4 Tsp Parsley, Leaves
➤ Pepper

- ➤ Pesto
- ➤ Salt
- ➤ 12 Shrimp, Jumbo

**Directions:**

1. Supply your smoker with wood pellets and follow the start-up procedure. Preheat the grill, with the lid closed, to 350° F. Place the baguette slices on a baking sheet lined with foil. Stir together the olive oil, and minced garlic, then brush both sides of the baguette slices with the mix. Place the pan inside the grill, and bake for about 10-15 minutes.

2. In a skillet, add a splash of olive oil, shrimp, chili powder, garlic powder, smoked paprika, salt pepper, and grill on medium-high heat for about 5 minutes (until the shrimp is pink). Be sure to stir often. Once pink, remove pan from heat. Once the baguettes are toasted, let them cool for 5 minutes, then spread a layer of pesto onto each one, then top with a shrimp, and serve.

# Smoked Fish Chowder

Servings: 4
Cooking Time: 60 Minutes

**Ingredients:**

- ➤ 12 Ounce (1-1/2 to 2 lb) skin-on salmon fillet, preferably wild-caught
- ➤ Fin & Feather Rub
- ➤ 2 Corn Husks
- ➤ 3 Slices Bacon, sliced
- ➤ 4 Can Cream of Potato Soup, Condensed
- ➤ 3 Cup whole milk
- ➤ 8 Ounce cream cheese
- ➤ 3 green onions, thinly sliced
- ➤ 2 Teaspoon hot sauce

**Directions:**

1. Supply your smoker with wood pellets and follow the start-up procedure. Preheat the grill, with the lid closed, to 180° F.

2. Sprinkle Traeger Fin & Feather rub as needed on salmon. Arrange the salmon skin-side down on the grill grate. Smoke for 30 minutes. Grill: 180 °F

3. Increase the grill temperature to 350°F. Grill: 350 °F

4. Cook the salmon for 30 minutes, or until the fish flakes easily with a fork. (The exact time will depend on the thickness of the fillet.) There is no need to turn the fish. Using a large thin spatula, transfer the salmon to a wire rack to cool. Remove the skin. (The salmon can be made a day ahead, wrapped in plastic wrap and refrigerated.) Break into flakes and set aside.

5. Arrange the corn and bacon strips on the grill grate. (The salmon will be roasting while you do this.) Roast the corn and the bacon until the corn is cooked through and browned in spots, turning as needed, and the bacon is crisp, about 15 minutes.

6. In the meantime, bring the cream of potato soup and the milk to a simmer over medium heat in a large saucepan or Dutch oven on the stovetop. Gradually stir in the cream cheese and whisk to blend. Chop the bacon into bits and slice the corn off the cobs using long strokes of a chef's knife.

7. Add to the soup along with the green onions. Stir in the salmon. Heat gently for 5 to 10 minutes. Add the hot sauce to taste. If the chowder is too thick, add more milk. Serve at once. Enjoy!

# Grilled Lemon Salmon

Servings: 4
Cooking Time: 60 Minutes

**Ingredients:**

- Dill, Fresh
- 1 Lemon, Sliced
- 1 1/2 - 2 Lbs Salmon, Fresh

**Directions:**

1. Supply your smoker with wood pellets and follow the start-up procedure. Preheat the grill, with the lid closed, to 225° F.
2. Place the salmon on a cedar plank. Lay the lemon slices along the top of the salmon. Smoke in your Grill for about 60 minutes.
3. Top with fresh dill and serve.

# Bacon Wrapped Scallops

Servings: 8
Cooking Time: 20 Minutes

**Ingredients:**

- 24 jumbo deep sea diver scallops, dry-packed
- 1/2 Cup butter
- salt
- freshly ground black pepper
- 1 Clove garlic, minced
- 12 Slices thin-cut bacon, cut in half crosswise
- lemon wedges, for serving

**Directions:**

1. Remove the small, crescent-shaped muscle from the side of each scallop, if still attached. Dry the scallops thoroughly on paper towels, then transfer to a medium bowl.
2. Melt butter in a small saucepan, add garlic and cook for 1 minute. Let cool slightly then pour over the scallops. Season with salt and pepper and gently toss to coat.

3. Wrap a piece of bacon around each scallop and secure with a toothpick.
4. Supply your smoker with wood pellets and follow the start-up procedure. Preheat the grill, with the lid closed, to 400° F.
5. Arrange the scallops directly on the grill grate. Grill for 15 to 20 minutes, or until the scallop is opaque and the bacon has begun to crisp. If desired, you can turn the scallops on their side, bacon-side down, turning occasionally to crisp the bacon. Do not overcook. Grill: 400 ˚F
6. Transfer the scallops to a platter and serve with lemon wedges.

# Cured Cold-smoked Lox

Servings: 6
Cooking Time: 360 Minutes

**Ingredients:**

- ¼ cup salt
- ¼ cup sugar
- 1 tablespoon freshly ground black pepper
- 1 bunch dill, chopped
- 1 pound sashimi-grade salmon, skin removed
- 1 avocado, sliced
- 8 bagels
- 4 ounces cream cheese
- 1 bunch alfalfa sprouts
- 1 (3.5-ounce) jar capers

**Directions:**

1. In a small bowl, combine the salt, sugar, pepper, and fresh dill to make the curing mixture. Set aside.
2. On a smooth surface, lay out a large piece of plastic wrap and spread half of the curing salt mixture in the middle, spreading it out to about the size of the salmon.
3. Place the salmon on top of the curing salt.

4. Top the fish with the remaining curing salt, covering it completely. Wrap the salmon, leaving the ends open to drain.

5. Place the wrapped fish in a rimmed baking pan or dish lined with paper towels to soak up liquid.

6. Place a weight on the salmon evenly, such as a pan with a couple of heavy jars of pickles on top.

7. Put the salmon pan with weights in the refrigerator. Place something (a dishtowel, for example) under the back of the pan in order to slightly tip it down so the liquid drains away from the fish.

8. Leave the salmon to cure in the refrigerator for 24 hours.

9. Place the wood pellets in the smoker, but do not follow the start-up procedure and do not preheat.

10. Remove the salmon from the refrigerator, unwrap it, rinse it off, and pat dry.

11. Put the salmon in the smoker while still cold from the refrigerator to slow down the cooking process. You'll need to use a cold-smoker attachment or enlist the help of a smoker tube to hold the temperature at 80°F and maintain that for 6 hours to absorb smoke and complete the cold-smoking process.

12. Remove the salmon from the smoker, place it in a sealed plastic bag, and refrigerate for 24 hours. The salmon will be translucent all the way through.

13. Thinly slice the lox and serve with sliced avocado, bagels, cream cheese, alfalfa sprouts, and capers.

# Smoked Honey Salmon

Servings: 2

Cooking Time: 25 Minutes

**Ingredients:**

➢ 1 lb. salmon fillets
➢ 1/2 tsp. pepper
➢ 1/4 tsp. salt
➢ 2 tbsp. sriracha
➢ 2 tsp. honey
➢ 2 tsp. chili sauce
➢ 1 tsp. lime juice
➢ 1/2 tsp. fish sauce

**Directions:**

1. Supply your smoker with wood pellets and follow the start-up procedure. Preheat the grill, with the lid closed, to 350° F.

2. Sprinkle the salmon with salt and pepper.

3. In a bowl, whisk together the sriracha, honey, chili sauce, lime juice, and fish sauce.

4. Once the grill is hot, place the salmon on the grill and leave for 15 minutes.

5. After 15 minutes, brush the salmon with the sriracha chili sauce and keep cooking for 5-10minutes. The salmon should be firm to the touch and crispy on the edges.

6. Serve hot!

# Grilled Artichoke Cheese Salmon

Servings: 12

Cooking Time: 270 Minutes

**Ingredients:**

➢ 28 Oz Artichoke Hearts, Whole, Canned
➢ 1/2 Cup Breadcrumbs
➢ 1/2 Cup Brown Sugar
➢ 8 Oz Cream Cheese
➢ 1 Tbsp Garlic Powder
➢ 1 Cup Italian Cheese Blend, Shredded
➢ 1/4 Cup Kosher Salt
➢ 1 Cup Mayonnaise

- ➤ 2 Tsp Olive Oil
- ➤ 1 Tbsp Onion Powder
- ➤ 1/2 Cup Parmesan Cheese
- ➤ 2 Tbsp Parsley, Chopped
- ➤ Blackened Sriracha Rub
- ➤ 1 1/4 Lbs Salmon, Fillet, Scaled And Deboned
- ➤ Sour Cream
- ➤ 1/2 Tsp White Pepper, Ground

**Directions:**

1. In a small mixing bowl, whisk together the brown sugar, salt, garlic powder, onion powder, and white pepper. This will make twice the cure needed, so be sure and place the remaining half in a resealable plastic bag and save for smoking fish at a later date.

2. Lay a sheet of plastic wrap on a sheet tray and sprinkle a thin layer of the cure on it. Place the salmon skin-side down on top of the cure, then sprinkle a couple tablespoons of cure on top. Gently press the cure on top of the salmon flesh, then wrap in plastic wrap.

3. Refrigerate for 8 hours, or overnight.

4. Remove salmon from the refrigerator and wash off the cure in the sink, under cold water.

5. Blot salmon with a paper towel, then set salmon skin side on a wire rack. Dry at room temperature for two hours, or until a yellowish shimmer appears on the salmon.

6. Supply your smoker with wood pellets and follow the start-up procedure. Preheat the grill, with the lid closed, to 250° F. If using a gas, charcoal or other grill, set it to low, indirect heat.

7. Place the salmon in the upper cabinet. Smoke for 2 hours, then increase the grill temperature to 350° F to maintain a cabinet temperature of 225°F and smoke another 1 to 2 hours, until salmon reaches an internal temperature of 145° F.

8. Remove salmon from the cabinet and set aside to rest for 15 minutes, then flake apart. Reserve ½ cup to top dip after grilling.

9. While the salmon is resting, drain the artichokes, then skewer onto metal skewers (if using wooden skewers, make sure to soak in water for 1 hour prior to grilling, or you can use a grill basket as well).

10. Season with Blackened Sriracha, then set on the grill. Grill for 2 to 3 minutes, until lightly browned.

11. Remove from the grill, cool slightly, then roughly chop. Set aside.

12. In a mixing bowl, combine shredded Italian cheese, grated parmesan, breadcrumbs and parsley. Set aside.

13. Place cream cheese, mayonnaise, and sour cream in a cast iron skillet. Stir frequently, with a wooden spoon, for about 5 minutes, until the mixture is smooth.

14. Carefully fold in flaked salmon and grilled artichoke hearts, then spread breadcrumb mixture over dip.

15. Drizzle with olive oil, then close the grill lid and bake for 25 to 30 minutes, until dip begins to bubble around the edges, and cheese begins to caramelize on top.

16. Remove dip from the grill, top with reserved salmon and a pinch of parsley. Serve warm with bagel chips, crackers, or crusty bread.

# Garlic Blackened Catfish

Servings: 4

Cooking Time: 10 Minutes

## Ingredients:

- ½ Cup Cajun Seasoning
- ¼ Tsp Cayenne Pepper
- 1 Tsp Granulated Garlic
- 1 Tsp Ground Thyme
- 1 Tsp Onion Powder
- 1 Tsp Ground Oregano
- 1 Tsp Pepper
- 4 (5-Oz.) Skinless Catfish Fillets
- 1 Tbsp Smoked Paprika
- 1 Stick Unsalted Butter

## Directions:

1. In a small bowl, combine the Cajun seasoning, smoked paprika, onion powder, granulated garlic, ground oregano, ground thyme, pepper and cayenne pepper.

2. Sprinkle fish with salt and let rest for 20 minutes.

3. Supply your smoker with wood pellets and follow the start-up procedure. Preheat the grill, with the lid closed, to 450° F. If you're using a gas or charcoal grill, set it up for medium-high heat. Place cast iron skillet on the grill and let it preheat.

4. While grill is preheating, sprinkle catfish fillets with seasoning mixture, pressing gently to adhere. Add half the butter to preheated cast iron skillet and swirl to coat, add more butter if needed. Place fillets in hot skillet and cook 3-5 minutes or until a dark crust has been formed. Flip and cook an additional 3-5 minutes or until the fish flakes apart when pressed gently with your finger.

5. Remove fish from grill and sprinkle evenly with fresh parsley. Serve with lemon wedges and enjoy!

# Grilled Tuna Steaks With Lemon & Caper Butter

Servings: 4

Cooking Time: 8 Minutes

## Ingredients:

- 4 tuna steaks, each about 8oz (225g) and 1 inch (2.5cm) thick
- extra virgin olive oil
- coarse salt
- freshly ground black pepper
- for the butter
- 6 tbsp unsalted butter, chilled, divided
- 1 garlic clove, peeled and minced
- 3 tbsp brined capers, drained and coarsely chopped
- 1 tbsp freshly squeezed lemon juice, plus more
- 1 tsp lemon zest
- 1 tbsp minced fresh chives or flat-leaf parsley

## Directions:

1. Supply your smoker with wood pellets and follow the start-up procedure. Preheat the grill, with the lid closed, to 450° F.

2. In a small saucepan on the stovetop over medium-low heat, begin making the butter by melting 1 tablespoon of butter. (Cut the remaining butter into ½-inch (1.25cm) cubes and keep them cold.) Add the garlic and capers. Cook until the garlic is softened, about 3 minutes. Stir in the lemon juice and zest. Remove the saucepan from the heat and set aside.

3. Lightly brush the tuna steaks with olive oil. Season with salt and pepper. Place the steaks on the grate and grill until seared, about 3 to 4

minutes per side. (The tuna will be quite rare in the center, almost like sashimi. If you prefer your tuna more well done, add 4 to 6 minutes to the grilling time.)

4. Transfer the steaks to a platter and let rest for 5 minutes.

5. Reheat the butter and caper mixture over low heat. Whisk in the chilled butter one or two cubes at a time until the sauce has emulsified. Stir in the chives. Ladle the sauce over the tuna. Serve immediately.

# Planked Trout With Fennel, Bacon & Orange

Servings: 4
Cooking Time: 40minutes

## Ingredients:

- ➢ 4 whole trout, each about 14 to 16oz (400 to 450g), cleaned and gutted, fins removed
- ➢ coarse salt
- ➢ freshly ground black pepper
- ➢ for the filling
- ➢ 1 large navel orange
- ➢ 4 slices of thick-cut bacon, diced
- ➢ 1 large fennel bulb, trimmed, halved, decored, and diced, green fronds reserved
- ➢ 4oz (110g) baby spinach, about 6 cups
- ➢ coarse salt
- ➢ freshly ground black pepper

## Directions:

1. Supply your smoker with wood pellets and follow the start-up procedure. Preheat the grill, with the lid closed, to 450° F. Place 4 cedar planks on the grate and allow them to singe slightly on both sides. Remove them from the grill and place them on a heatproof surface to cool.

2. Lower the temperature to 300°F (149°C).

3. Slice 4 thin rounds from the center of the orange and then slice each in half for 8 pieces total. Zest the remainder of the orange and set aside.

4. In a cold skillet on the stovetop over medium heat, sauté the bacon, until the fat has rendered and the bacon is golden brown, about 6 to 8 minutes, stirring frequently. Use a slotted spoon to transfer the bacon to paper towels to drain. Add the fennel to the fat in the skillet and cook until tender crisp, about 5 minutes. Add the spinach and stir until it wilts, about 1 to 2 minutes. Squeeze the juice of one of the reserved orange ends over the mixture. Add the drained bacon. Season with salt and pepper and then stir. Remove the skillet from the stovetop and set aside.

5. Rinse each trout inside and out under cold running water and pat dry with paper towels. Place three 12-inch (30.5cm) pieces of butcher's twine on each plank and place a trout on top. Season the inside of each fish with salt and pepper. Place two half-rounds of orange in each belly, rind side facing out. Top with some of the filling. Tie the trout with the butcher's twine and trim any ends. Repeat with the remaining trout.

6. Place the planks on the grate and cook the trout until they're cooked through, about 30 to 40 minutes.

7. Remove the planks from the grill and remove the twine. Top each trout with a few curls of orange zest and some reserved fennel fronds. Serve the trout on the planks.

# PORK RECIPES

## Grilled Rosemary Pork Chops

Servings: 4

Cooking Time: 10 Minutes

**Ingredients:**

- 6 Tbsp Brown Sugar
- 4 Pork, Chop
- 2 Tbsp Dried Rosemary, Springs
- 1 Cup Soy Sauce
- 1/2 Cup Water, Warm

**Directions:**

1. Supply your smoker with wood pellets and follow the start-up procedure. Preheat the grill, with the lid open, to 350° F.

2. Lightly oil the grate. Remove the pork chops from the marinade, shake off the excess, and discard the marinade.

3. Grill the pork chops until the pork is no longer pink in the center, while brushing occasionally with the reserved marinade, for about 4-5 minutes on each side, or until done.

4. Remove the pork chops from the grill and serve.

## Cheese Potato Stuffed Pork Chops

Servings: 4

Cooking Time: 45 Minutes

**Ingredients:**

- 4 Bone-In Pork Chops
- 1 Package Frozen Shredded Hash Browns, Thawed
- 1 Tbsp Parsley, Minced Fresh
- Pulled Pork Seasoning
- 1 Cup Shredded Cheddar Cheese
- ¼ Cup Sour Cream
- White Onion, Diced

**Directions:**

1. Place the pork chops on a flat work surface. Using a sharp knife, cut a pocket into the side of each pork chop, being careful not to cut all the way through the sides of the chop. Season the pork chops generously on both sides with Pulled Pork Seasoning.

2. In a large mixing bowl, mix together the hash browns, shredded cheddar, sour cream, diced onion, parsley, and 1 tablespoon of Pulled Pork seasoning. Stuff each pork chop with about ¼ cup of the potato filling. Use a toothpick to securely close the chop if needed.

3. Supply your smoker with wood pellets and follow the start-up procedure. Preheat the grill, with the lid open, to 350° F. If you're using a gas or charcoal grill, set it up for medium heat. Insert a temperature probe into the thickest part of one of the chops and place the meat on the grill. Grill the chops on one side for 10-15 minutes, then flip and grill for another 10-15, or until the internal temperature of the chops reach 145°F.

4. Remove the chops from the grill, take the toothpicks out of the meat, and serve immediately.

## Korean Pulled Pork Lettuce Wraps

Servings: 8

Cooking Time: 480 Minutes

**Ingredients:**

- 1 bone-in pork shoulder, about 6lb (2.7kg)

- 1 cup low-carb beer or sugar-free light-colored soda
- for the sauce
- 1½ cups low-carb barbecue sauce
- ¼ cup low-carb beer or sugar-free light- or dark-colored soda
- 3 tbsp gochujang
- 3 tbsp light soy sauce
- 1 tbsp rice wine vinegar
- 1 tbsp toasted Asian sesame oil
- 1 tsp gochugaru
- for the rub
- 3 tbsp coarse salt
- 3 tbsp gochugaru
- 3 tbsp granulated light brown sugar or low-carb substitute
- 2 tsp granulated garlic
- 2 tsp onion powder
- 1 tsp ground ginger

**Directions:**

1. Supply your smoker with wood pellets and follow the start-up procedure. Preheat the grill, with the lid closed, to 250° F.

2. In a small bowl, make the barbecue sauce by whisking together the ingredients. Cover and refrigerate until ready to serve.

3. In a small bowl, make the rub by combining the ingredients. Rinse the meat with cold running water and pat dry with paper towels. Sprinkle the rub evenly over the surface, using your fingertips to pat it on.

4. Place the pork shoulder on the grate and smoke until the internal temperature reaches 165°F (74°C), about 4 to 5 hours. Transfer the meat to an aluminum foil roasting pan. Add the beer and then cover the pan tightly with heavy-duty aluminum foil. Continue to cook until the internal temperature reaches 200°F (93°C), about 3 hours more. (Keep the probe from touching bone or it will give you a false reading.) When the pork is tender enough to pull, the meat will release easily from the bone.

5. Transfer the pork shoulder to a cutting board. Drain the accumulated juices into a separate container and reserve. While the pork is still hot, pull out the bone and separate the meat into chunks. Using meat claws, forks, or your fingers, pull the meat into shreds, discarding any lumps of fat or undesirable bits. Return the meat to the pan. Stir in some of the reserved cooking juices if desired. You want the pork to be moist but not soupy.

6. Wrap the hot pork in lettuce leaves. Top with thinly sliced garlic, thinly sliced crosswise jalapeños, toasted sesame seeds, pickled ginger, and barbecue sauce. You can also serve the pork the American way: piled high on sesame seed buns.

# Old-fashioned Roasted Glazed Ham

Servings: 8
Cooking Time: 60 Minutes

**Ingredients:**

- 1 (10 lb) fully cooked bone-in spiral cut ham
- 1 Cup pineapple juice
- 1/2 Cup brown sugar
- 1 cinnamon stick
- 14 whole cloves
- 1 Whole Pineapple, fresh
- 10 Cherries, fresh, sweet

**Directions:**

1. Supply your smoker with wood pellets and follow the start-up procedure. Preheat the grill, with the lid closed, to 325° F.

2. Rinse ham under cold water and pat dry with paper towel.

3. In a saucepan combine pineapple juice, brown sugar, cinnamon stick and four cloves. Bring to a boil. Reduce heat to medium low and simmer for about 15 minutes or until pineapple juice is reduced by half, thick and syrupy.

4. Brush half of the glaze onto the ham and into the folds of the cut slices. Reserve the other half of the glaze for later.

5. Cut pineapple in desired sized pieces, about 2 inch squares, then place on ham with a cherry and a clove to pin in place, repeating all over ham.

6. Put ham in a deep baking dish with fat side up. Place on the Traeger and cook for about 1-¼ hours. Grill: 325 ˚F

7. Carefully remove from Traeger and brush remaining glaze onto ham.

8. Return ham to Traeger and continue cooking for another 15 to 20 minutes, until internal temperature of ham reaches 160°F. Grill: 325 ˚F Probe: 160 ˚F

9. Allow ham to rest for 15 – 20 minutes before serving. Enjoy!

# Maple-smoked Pork Chops

Servings: 4

Cooking Time: 55 Minutes

**Ingredients:**
➢ 1 (12-pound) full packer brisket
➢ 2 tablespoons yellow mustard
➢ 1 batch Espresso Brisket Rub
➢ Worcestershire Mop and Spritz, for spritzing

**Directions:**

1. Supply your smoker with wood pellets and follow the start-up procedure. Preheat the grill, with the lid closed, to 180°F.

2. Season the pork chops on both sides with salt and pepper.

3. Place the chops directly on the grill grate and smoke for 30 minutes.

4. Increase the grill's temperature to 350°F. Continue to cook the chops until their internal temperature reaches 145°F.

5. Remove the pork chops from the grill and let them rest for 5 minutes before serving.

# Smoked Pork Tomato Tamales

Servings: 6-8

Cooking Time: 60 Minutes

**Ingredients:**
➢ 1 Boneless, Netted Pork Roast
➢ 1 Cup, Fresh Cilantro, Chopped
➢ 3 Cloves Garlic, Peeled
➢ 20 Dried Cornhusks
➢ 1 Tbsp Lime Juice
➢ ¼ Cup Olive Oil
➢ 1 Onion, Quartered
➢ 4 - 6 Cups Prepared Masa Harina Tamale Dough
➢ 3 – 4 Serrano Peppers, Deseeded
➢ 1 Tbsp Sweet Heat Rub
➢ 1 Lb. Tomatillos, Husked And Washed

**Directions:**

1. Began by soaking the corn husks in a pan filled with water. Soak for 2 – 4 hours, or if needed, overnight.

2. Unwrap the tomatillos from their shell and place all of them into a grill basket followed by a few Serranos, deseeded, garlic cloves and 1 onion cut into quarters.

3. Supply your smoker with wood pellets and follow the start-up procedure. Preheat the grill, with the lid open, to 400° F. If you're using a gas or charcoal grill, set it up for medium low heat, and use smoke chips to fill your grill with smoke for 15 minutes. Place the grill basket filled with your vegetables and roast them over an open flame on your smoker until vegetables have become charred.

4. Place tomatillos, peppers, garlic and onions in a bowl, cover with plastic wrap, and let stand until cool enough to handle, 10 to 15 minutes.

5. Season the pork roast generously with Sweet Heat Rub and grill at 350°F for 1 hour until the roast has a nice crust on the outside.

6. While the pork roast is cooking, add a handful of cilantro, charred vegetables, 1 tbsp of Sweet Heat Rub, 1 tbsp lime juice, and ¼ cup of olive oil to a food processor. Pulse in food processor until mixture is consistent. Set aside

7. After the pork roast has been grilled for an hour, turn heat down to 275°F. Put roast in pan with about a cup of water, cover with aluminum foil and cook for another 4 hours or until the roast can be shredded. Pour chile verde sauce over shredded pork and toss to combine.

8. To being assembling tamales, place a corn husk on a work surface. Place 2-3 tablespoons of tamale dough on larger end of husk and spread into a rectangle, about ¼" thick, leaving a small border along the edge. Place large tablespoon of chili and pork filling on top of dough. Fold over sides of husk so dough surrounds filling, then fold bottom of husk up and secure closed by tying a thin strip of husk around tamale.

9. To cook tamales, place them in a large metal colander over a large stockpot filled with water. Cover and let steam for 1 hour. After the tamales have been steamed, take them off and grill them at 350°F for about 10-20 minutes until corn husks have charred marks.

# Beer Braised Garlic Bbq Pork Butt

Servings: 6-8
Cooking Time: 300 Minutes

**Ingredients:**
➢ One 12Oz Bottle Dark Beer
➢ 1/2 Cup Brown Sugar
➢ 2 Tablespoons Granulated Garlic
➢ 4 Tablespoons Honey
➢ 1 Cup Ketchup
➢ 1 Tablespoon Olive Oil
➢ Pulled Pork Rub
➢ 1 Pork Butt, Boneless
➢ 2 Tablespoons Worcestershire Sauce
➢ 4 Tablespoons Yellow Mustard

**Directions:**
1. Generously season the pork butt with Pulled Pork Rub, making sure to rub the seasoning in on all surfaces of roast. Place the pork onto a roasting rack inside a 9x13 pan.

2. Pour about half a bottle of dark beer into the bottom of the pan and save the remaining amount of beer, you'll need this later.

3. Supply your smoker with wood pellets and follow the start-up procedure. Preheat the grill, with the lid open, to high heat. If you're using a gas or charcoal, set it up for high direct heat. Place the pan in the center of the grill and grill for 30 minutes until the pork roast is dark in color and charred in some spots.

4. Remove the pork from the grill and decrease the temperature of the grill to 325°F. Set aside and began to make the BBQ sauce.

5. In a medium sized bowl, add ketchup, brown sugar, yellow mustard, honey, Worcestershire, granulated garlic, half bottle of dark beer, and finally 1 tbsp of Pulled Pork Rub. Mix together thoroughly.

6. Take the sauce and pour it over the roast, cover with aluminum foil.

7. Cook the roast for 4 - 6 hours or until the meat is falling apart tender and the bone easily comes away from the meat and reaches an internal temperature of 200°F. Remove the pork from the grill and allow it to rest for 10-15 minutes.

8. Shred the pork with meat claws or forks, discarding any fat or gristle. Toss the shredded pork with the barbecue sauce and serve immediately.

# Classic Pulled Pork

Servings: 8-12

Cooking Time: 1200 Minutes

## Ingredients:

➢ 1 (6- to 8-pound) bone-in pork shoulder
➢ 2 tablespoons yellow mustard
➢ 1 batch Pork Rub

## Directions:

1. Supply your smoker with wood pellets and follow the start-up procedure. Preheat the grill, with the lid closed, to 225°F.

2. Coat the pork shoulder all over with mustard and season it with the rub. Using your hands, work the rub into the meat.

3. Place the shoulder on the grill grate and smoke until its internal temperature reaches 195°F.

4. Pull the shoulder from the grill and wrap it completely in aluminum foil or butcher paper. Place it in a cooler, cover the cooler, and let it rest for 1 or 2 hours.

5. Remove the pork shoulder from the cooler and unwrap it. Remove the shoulder bone and pull the pork apart using just your fingers. Serve immediately as desired. Leftovers are encouraged.

# Grilled St. Louis Style Ribs With Tequila Bbq

Servings: 8

Cooking Time: 240 Minutes

## Ingredients:

➢ 1/2 Cup Brown Sugar
➢ 2 Garlic, Cloves
➢ 3 Tbsp Honey
➢ 1 Cup Ketchup
➢ 1/2 Squeezed Lime
➢ 3 Tbsp Molasses
➢ 1 Jar Mustard
➢ 2 Slabs Slabs St. Louis-Style Rib Racks
➢ 1 Bottle Sweet Heat Rub
➢ 1/4 Cup Tequila Blanco

## Directions:

1. First, make the barbecue sauce. In a mixing bowl, add the ketchup, brown sugar, garlic cloves, molasses, honey, tequila, lime, and 1 tbsp Sweet Heat Rub. Mix together well until glaze is blended together. Set aside.

2. Prepare the ribs. Pat the ribs dry with paper towels, then pull the thin membrane off the back of the ribs and discard. Using a basting brush, coat the meat on both sides with a thin layer of

mustard and season heavily with Sweet Heat Rub until the ribs are completely coated. Repeat with the second rack of ribs. Place the ribs on a baking sheet and refrigerate overnight, or for 12 hours if you choose to.

3. Once the ribs have finished marinating, remove them from the refrigerator and set out two sheets of large, heavy duty aluminum foil. Place one rack of ribs on each sheet of foil, meat-side down, and fold the edges over to form a sealed pouch.

4. Supply your smoker with wood pellets and follow the start-up procedure. Preheat the grill, with the lid open, to 225° F. If you're using a gas or charcoal grill, set it up for low, indirect heat. Place the rib packets on the grill, meat-side up, and smoke for 2-3 hours, or until the ribs are nearly tender.

5. Remove the ribs from the grill and take the aluminum foil off the ribs and place them back onto the grill for another hour. Brush generously with the tequila barbecue sauce on both sides, then grill for 5 minutes, meat- side up. Baste the ribs one more time with the barbecue sauce, then flip them meat-side down and grill for a final 5 minutes. The ribs should be sticky and caramelized. Remove the ribs from the grill and serve immediately with the remaining barbecue sauce.

# Spiced Pulled Pork Shoulder

Servings: 16
Cooking Time: 600 Minutes

## Ingredients:
➤ 5-8 lb Bone-in Pork Shoulder
➤ Maple Chili Rub
➤ Maple Sugar
➤ Kosher Salt
➤ Fresh Ground Black Pepper
➤ Roasted Garlic Powder
➤ Onion Powder
➤ Cumin
➤ Chipotle Powder
➤ Chili Powder
➤ Cinnamon Powder

## Directions:
1. Supply your smoker with wood pellets and follow the start-up procedure. Preheat the grill, with the lid closed, to 225° F. Using apple pellets for this dish will impart a slightly sweeter smoke that goes great with the rub.

2. In a bowl combine rub ingredients.

3. Trim excess fat from pork shoulder, score fat with a sharp knife (only slice about 1/8" into pork), then cover with rub. Reserve some rub to be sprinkled on the meat after it has been shredded.

4. Place the pork onto the smoker.

5. Continue to smoke pork until internal temperature reaches 203 °F, about 10 hours. You can wrap pork in butcher paper once it reaches 160 °F if you want to speed up cooking time (your final bark won't be as good though).

6. Once Pork reaches 203 °F, remove from smoker then wrap tightly in aluminum foil. Place wrapped Pork into a cooler for 1 hour.

7. After 1 hour remove pork from the foil, pull out the bones, using 2 forks shred the pork to your desired consistency.

8. Sprinkle left over rub onto the pork and toss to coat.

9. Enjoy!

# Bacon Onion Ring

Servings: 6
Cooking Time: 60 Minutes

**Ingredients:**

- 16 Slices bacon
- 2 Whole Vidalia onion, sliced
- 1 Tablespoon Chili Garlic Sauce
- 1 Tablespoon yellow mustard
- 1 Teaspoon honey

**Directions:**

1. Wrap a piece of bacon around an individual onion ring; continue until bacon is gone. Some onion slices may be larger and require 2 pieces of bacon to complete a ring.
2. Place a skewer through the bacon-wrapped onion slice, to keep bacon from unraveling while cooking.
3. Supply your smoker with wood pellets and follow the start-up procedure. Preheat the grill, with the lid closed, to 400° F.
4. Meanwhile, mix chili garlic sauce and yellow mustard in a small bowl until incorporated; add honey.
5. Place skewers on the grill grate and cook for approximately 90 minutes, flipping after 45 minutes. Enjoy! Grill: 400 °F

# Bbq Pulled Coleslaw Pork Sandwiches

Servings: 12
Cooking Time: 480 Minutes

**Ingredients:**

- 1 Bottle Bbq Sauce
- Coleslaw, Prepared
- 12 Kaiser Rolls
- 8-10Lbs Pork Butt Roast, Bone-In

- 5 Oz Sugar
- 1 Cup Yellow Mustard

**Directions:**

1. Supply your smoker with wood pellets and follow the start-up procedure. Preheat the grill, with the lid open, to 225° F. While your grill is heating, remove the pork roast from its packaging and place on a cookie sheet. Rub the pork roast down with yellow mustard.
2. Mix BBQ sauce and sugar in a bowl. Rub the roast down with entire mixture, allowing time for the rub to melt into the meat.
3. Place the roast in the smoker and cook for 6 hours.
4. After 6 hours, remove the roast and double wrap in tin foil. Turn the grill up to 250°F and cook the roast for another 2 hours or until the roast is probe tender (around an internal temperature of 204°F). Let the pork butt rest in the foil for up to an hour before pulling.
5. Cut each Kaiser roll in half, mix pulled pork with some more barbecue sauce and pile on each half of roll. Top with coleslaw and green onions. Don't mix all the pulled pork with barbecue sauce so that you can use the extra pulled pork for different recipes. Serve hot and enjoy!

# Crown Roast Of Pork

Servings: 4
Cooking Time: 60 Minutes

**Ingredients:**

- 1 Whole Crown Roast of Pork, 12-14 ribs
- 1/4 Cup Pork & Poultry Rub
- 1 Cup apple juice
- 1 Cup Apricot BBQ Sauce

**Directions:**

1. Supply your smoker with wood pellets and follow the start-up procedure. Preheat the grill, with the lid closed, to 375° F.

2. Season the pork roast liberally with Traeger Pork and Poultry Rub. Let sit at room temperature for 30 minutes. Wrap each tip of the crown roast in a small piece of aluminum foil. This will protect the bones during the cook and prevent them from turning black.

3. Place the roast directly on the grill grate and cook for about 90 minutes spraying with apple juice every 30 minutes or so.

4. When the roast reaches an internal temperature of 125 degrees F, remove the aluminum foil from the bones and return to the grill.

5. Spray again with apple juice and continue to cook until the internal temperature reaches 135 degrees F in the thickest part of the roast. In the last ten minutes, baste the roast with the Apricot BBQ Sauce to let the glaze set.

6. Remove from the grill, tent with foil, and let it rest 15-20 minutes before slicing. Enjoy!

## Hot & Fast Smoked Baby Back Ribs

Servings: 6
Cooking Time: 180 Minutes

**Ingredients:**
➢ 3 Rack baby back ribs
➢ Pork & Poultry Rub
➢ 2 Cup apple juice

**Directions:**
1. Supply your smoker with wood pellets and follow the start-up procedure. Preheat the grill, with the lid closed, to 300° F.

2. Pull membrane from back of the ribs and trim any excess fat.

3. Season front and back of ribs with the Traeger Pork & Poultry Rub. Let rest on counter for 10 minutes. Grill: 300 °F

4. Place ribs directly on the grill and cook for 30 minutes. Grill: 300 °F

5. While ribs cook, put apple juice in a spray bottle. Spray ribs with apple juice after the first 30 minutes of cooking and every 30 minutes after, about 2-1/2 hours. Grill: 300 °F Probe: 202 °F

6. Check the internal temperature of the ribs. The desired temperature is 202°F. If the desired temperature has not been reached, check every 20 minutes until it comes to temperature. Grill: 300 °F Probe: 202 °F

7. Remove ribs from grill and let rest 10 minutes before slicing and serving. Enjoy!

## Competition Style Bbq Pulled Pork

Servings: 8
Cooking Time: 600 Minutes

**Ingredients:**
➢ 1 (8-10 lb) bone-in pork butt
➢ 1 Cup Pork & Poultry Rub, divided
➢ 2 3/4 Cup apple juice, divided
➢ 1/4 Cup Butcher BBQ Pork Injection
➢ meat injector

**Directions:**
1. Supply your smoker with wood pellets and follow the start-up procedure. Preheat the grill, with the lid closed, to 225° F.

2. While the grill heats up, trim excess fat from pork.

3. In a small bowl, mix together half the Traeger Pork & Poultry Rub, 2 cups apple juice and

butchers pork injection. Thoroughly inject pork butt throughout using an injector.

4. Season the pork with a layer of Traeger Pork & Poultry Rub. Let pork rest for 20 minutes.

5. Place pork on the grill and cook for 4-1/2 to 5-1/2 hours. After 4-1/2 hours, check the internal temperature of the pork. It should be between 155-165°F. If not, check again in 30 minutes. Grill: 225 °F Probe: 155 °F

6. When the temperature reaches 155-165°F, wrap the pork in a double layer of heavy duty aluminum foil. Pour 3/4 cup reserved apple juice in a foil packet with the pork and place back on the grill.

7. Turn the grill temperature up to 250°F and cook for another 3 to 4 hours. Check the internal temperature after 3 hours. The desired temperature is between 204°F and 206°F in the thickest part of the pork. If the pork is not to temperature, check back every 30 minutes until it reaches 204-206°F. The entire cook time should be between 8-10 hours depending on the size of the pork. Grill: 250 °F Probe: 204 °F

8. Remove pork from grill and open the foil packet to vent for 10 minutes. Seal back up and let rest for 45 minutes to one hour.

9. After resting, pour the liquid out of the foil and separate the fat from the broth using a fat separator. Remove the bone and pull the meat. Add 2 cups of the broth to the pulled meat. Add extra broth, if necessary, to achieve desired moisture level. Enjoy!

# Bbq Sweet & Smoky Ribs

Servings: 6
Cooking Time: 300 Minutes

**Ingredients:**

- ➤ 2 Rack Pork, Spare Ribs Trimmed
- ➤ 6 Cup apple juice
- ➤ 2 Tablespoon Big Game Rub
- ➤ 2 Cup 'Que BBQ Sauce
- ➤ 1/4 Cup brown sugar

**Directions:**

1. If your butcher has not already done so, remove the thin papery membrane from the bone-side of the ribs by working the tip of a butter knife underneath the membrane over a middle bone. Use paper towels to get a firm grip, then tear the membrane off.

2. Lay the ribs in a baking dish. Pour the apple juice over ribs, using as much apple juice as needed to submerge the meaty side of the ribs. Turn to coat.

3. Cover and refrigerate ribs for 4 to 6 hours or overnight. Remove the ribs from the apple juice; reserve juice.

4. Sprinkle ribs on all sides with Traeger Big Game Rub.

5. Supply your smoker with wood pellets and follow the start-up procedure. Preheat the grill, with the lid closed, to 225° F.

6. Transfer the apple juice to a saucepan and place in a corner of the grill, the juice will keep the cooking environment moist.

7. Arrange the ribs bone side down, directly on the grill grate. Cook for 4 to 5 hours, or until a skewer or paring knife inserted between the bones goes in easily.

8. Check the internal temperature of the ribs, the desired temperature is 202°F. If not at temperature, cook for an additional 30 minutes or until temperature is reached.

9. Meanwhile, combine the BBQ sauce and brown sugar in a small saucepan. Generously

brush the ribs on all sides with the BBQ sauce the last hour of cooking

10. Using a sharp knife, cut the slabs into individual ribs. Serve. Enjoy!

# Unique Carolina Mustard Ribs

Servings: 4
Cooking Time: 300 Minutes

**Ingredients:**

➢ 1 Rack St. Louis Style Ribs
➢ 2 Cups Apple Juice
➢ 1/4 Cup Cider Vinegar
➢ 1/4 Cup Dark Brown Sugar
➢ 1/4 Cup Honey
➢ 1 Tablespoon Hot Sauce
➢ 2 Tablespoons Ketchup
➢ 7 Tablespoon Sweet Rib Rub
➢ 1 Tablespoon Worcestershire Sauce
➢ 2 Cups, Prepared Yellow Mustard

**Directions:**

1. Make the sauce for the ribs. In a large mixing bowl, combine 1 cup of the yellow mustard, cider vinegar, dark brown sugar, honey, ketchup, Worcestershire sauce, hot sauce, and 1 tablespoon of the Sweet Rib Rub. Mix well to combine and set in the refrigerator until ready to use.

2. Make the ribs. Using a paper towel, peel the membrane off of the backs of the rib racks and discard. Generously coat the ribs in a thin coat of mustard, and sprinkle all over with Sweet Rib Rub.

3. Supply your smoker with wood pellets and follow the start-up procedure. Preheat the grill, with the lid closed, to 275° F. If you're using a gas or charcoal grill set it up for low, indirect heat. Place the ribs meaty-side up and grill for 2-3 hours. Once the ribs have grilled for 2-3 hours,

fill a spray bottle with 2 cups of apple juice and spray the ribs to keep them moist. Continue to grill the ribs, spraying every 45 minutes, until the meat bends slightly at the ends when lifted and is a deep mahogany color, about another 2-3 hours.

4. Remove the ribs from the grill and brush with mustard sauce, then slice and serve immediately.

# Smoked Porchetta With Italian Salsa Verde

Servings: 8-12
Cooking Time: 180 Minutes

**Ingredients:**

➢ 3 Tablespoon dried fennel seed
➢ 2 Tablespoon red pepper flakes
➢ 2 Tablespoon sage, minced
➢ 1 Tablespoon rosemary, minced
➢ 3 Clove garlic, minced
➢ As Needed lemon zest
➢ As Needed orange zest
➢ To Taste salt and pepper
➢ 6 Pound Pork Belly, skin on
➢ As Needed salt and pepper
➢ 1 Whole shallot, thinly sliced
➢ 6 Tablespoon parsley, minced
➢ 2 Tablespoon freshly minced chives
➢ 1 Tablespoon Oregano, fresh
➢ 3 Tablespoon white wine vinegar
➢ 1/2 Teaspoon kosher salt
➢ 3/4 Cup olive oil
➢ 1/2 Teaspoon Dijon mustard
➢ As Needed fresh lemon juice

**Directions:**

1. Prepare herb mixture: In a medium bowl, mix together fennel seeds, red pepper flakes, sage, rosemary, garlic, citrus zest, salt and pepper.

2. Place pork belly skin side up on a clean work surface and score in a crosshatch pattern. Flip the pork belly over and season flesh side with salt, pepper and half of the herb mixture.

3. Place trimmed pork loin in the center of the belly and rub with remaining herb mixture. Season with salt and pepper.

4. Roll the pork belly around the loin to form a cylindrical shape and tie tightly with kitchen twine at 1" intervals.

5. Season the outside with salt and pepper and transfer to refrigerator, uncovered and let air dry overnight.

6. When ready to cook, start the smoker grill and set to Smoke.

7. Fit a rimmed baking sheet with a rack and place the pork on the rack seam side down.

8. Place the pan directly on the grill grate and smoke for 1 hour.

9. Increase the grill temperature to 325 degrees F and roast until the internal temperature of the meat reaches 135 degrees, about 2 1/2 hours. If the exterior begins to burn before the desired internal temperature is reached, tent with foil.

10. Remove from grill and let stand 30 minutes before slicing.

11. To make the Italian salsa verde: Combine shallot, parsley, chives, vinegar, oregano and salt in a medium bowl. Whisk in olive oil then stir in mustard and lemon juice.

12. Drizzle slices with Italian salsa verde and enjoy!

# Hawaiian Pineapple Pork Butt

Servings: 8 - 10

Cooking Time: 720 Minutes

**Ingredients:**

➢ 6 - 8 Pineapple Rings
➢ 2 Cups Pineapple, Juice
➢ 1 8-10Lb Pork Butt Roast, Bone-In
➢ ¼ Cup Sweet Heat Rub

**Directions:**

1. Supply your smoker with wood pellets and follow the start-up procedure. Preheat the grill, with the lid open, to 225° F. If not using a pellet smoker, set up the smoker for indirect smoking.

2. Remove the pork butt from its packaging and drain any excess liquid from the pork butt. Pat the pork butt dry with paper towels and discard the paper towels.

3. Generously season the pork butt with the Sweet Heat seasoning, making sure that the roast is coated on all sides.

4. Place the pineapple rings evenly over the pork shoulder, fat side up, and pin with toothpicks. Place the pork butt into the 9x13 pan and pour the pineapple juice over the top.

5. Set the pan into the smoker. Make sure that the pork butt is placed as close to the center of the rack as possible for even cooking.

6. Place a temperature probe into the thickest part of the pork butt, and smoke the pork until it reaches an internal temperature of 201°F. The pork should be deeply browned and smell very porky.

7. Once the pork butt reaches its internal temperature, remove the pork butt from the grill and wrap it tightly in foil. Allow the roast to rest for at least 1 hour before shredding.

8. After the roast has rested for an hour, shred the pork with your meat claws, discarding any large chunks of fat. Serve immediately.

# Bacon-draped Injected Pork Loin Roast

Servings: 4
Cooking Time: 180 Minutes

## Ingredients:

- ➤ 1 Cup apple juice
- ➤ 1/4 Cup water
- ➤ 1 Teaspoon salt
- ➤ 1 Teaspoon Worcestershire sauce
- ➤ 3 Pound (3 lb) center-cut pork loin
- ➤ Sweet Rub
- ➤ 10 Slices bacon

## Directions:

1. In a small bowl combine apple juice, water, salt, and Worcestershire; stir to dissolve the salt crystals.Plunge the injector into the sauce and retract the needle to draw up the liquid. Liberally inject the meat.

2. Plunge the injector into the sauce and retract the needle to draw up the liquid. Liberally inject the meat.

3. Season the meat all over with the Traeger Sweet Rub.

4. Supply your smoker with wood pellets and follow the start-up procedure. Preheat the grill, with the lid closed, to 225° F.

5. Drape the loin with the bacon slices. Put the roast directly on the grill grate and smoke for 3 to 4 hours, or until the internal temperature of the meat is at least 145 degrees F on an instant-read thermometer. Grill: 225 ˚F Probe: 145 ˚F

6. Transfer the pork to a cutting board and let rest for 10 minutes before carving and serving. Enjoy!

# Smoked Bbq Ribs

Servings: 4
Cooking Time: 300 Minutes

## Ingredients:

- ➤ 2 Rack St. Louis-style ribs
- ➤ 1/4 Cup  Big Game Rub
- ➤ 1 Cup apple juice
- ➤ BBQ Sauce

## Directions:

1. Pat ribs dry and peel the membrane from the back of the ribs.

2. Apply an even coat of rub to the front, back and sides of the ribs. Let sit for 20 minutes and up to 4 hours if refrigerated.

3. Supply your smoker with wood pellets and follow the start-up procedure. Preheat the grill, with the lid closed, to 225° F.

4. Place ribs, bone side down on grill. Put apple juice in a spray bottle and spray the ribs after 1 hour of cooking. Spray every 45 minutes thereafter. Grill: 225 ˚F Probe: 201 ˚F

5. After 4-1/2 hours, check the internal temperature of ribs. Ribs are done when internal temperature reaches 201˚F. If not, check back in another 30 minutes. Grill: 225 ˚F Probe: 201 ˚F

6. Once ribs are done, brush a light layer of your favorite Traeger BBQ Sauce on the front and back of the ribs. Let the sauce set for 10 minutes. After the sauce has set, take ribs off the grill and let rest for 10 minutes. Slice ribs in between the bones and serve with extra sauce. Enjoy!

# Asian-style Pork Tenderloin

Servings: 6

Cooking Time: 15 Minutes

**Ingredients:**

- 2 Whole Pork Tenderloin, 8-10 oz each
- 2 Tablespoon canola oil
- 2 Tablespoon Sambai Oelek
- 1 Teaspoon sesame oil
- 1 Teaspoon garlic, minced
- 1 Teaspoon fresh ginger
- 1 Teaspoon fish sauce
- 1 Teaspoon soy sauce
- 1/4 Cup brown sugar

**Directions:**

1. Use a sharp paring knife to remove the silver skin of the pork tenderloin.

2. Combine all the ingredients together. Cover the tenderloins in the mixture and allow them to marinate in the refrigerator for 30 minutes.

3. Supply your smoker with wood pellets and follow the start-up procedure. Preheat the grill, with the lid closed, to 450° F.

4. Place the loins towards the very front of the grill; turn periodically until there are dark grill marks all around. Transfer them to the middle of the grill to finish cooking. Cook for an addition 7-10 minutes for a medium rare tenderloin. When they are done cooking, remove them from the grill and let them rest for 10 minutes before slicing. Enjoy!

# Braised Pork Carnitas

Servings: 6

Cooking Time: 180 Minutes

**Ingredients:**

- 2 Tbsp Bacon Fat Or Olive Oil
- 1 Cup Chicken Stock
- Cilantro, Chopped
- Corn Tortillas
- 3 Jalapeno Pepper, Minced
- 1 Lime, Wedges
- 2 Tbsp Pulled Pork Rub
- 3 Lbs Pork Shoulder, Boneless, Cut Into 1 ½ To 2 Inch Cubes
- Queso Fresco, Crumbled
- Red Onion, Minced

**Directions:**

1. Supply your smoker with wood pellets and follow the start-up procedure. Preheat the grill, with the lid open, to 300° F. If using a gas or charcoal grill, set it up for medium-low heat.

2. Season cubed pork shoulder with Pulled Pork Rub, then transfer to a cast iron Dutch oven, and add chicken stock. Transfer to center of grill with sear slide open. Bring mixture to a boil, then cover and close the sear slide. Simmer pork for 2 ½ hours, until tender.

3. Remove the lid and open the sear slide. Bring to boil and reduce liquid by half, about 15 minutes. Remove from grill and set aside.

4. Heat 1 tablespoon of bacon fat in the skillet, then use a slotted spoon to transfer the pork to the skillet. Fry pork in fat, stirring occasionally, for 8 to 10 minutes, until pork crisps up. Remove from grill.

5. Serve pork carnitas warm in fresh corn tortillas, with cilantro, red onion, jalapeño, queso fresco, and fresh lime.

# Competition Style Bbq Pork Ribs

Servings: 6
Cooking Time: 300 Minutes

**Ingredients:**

➢ 2 Rack St. Louis-style ribs
➢ 1 Cup Pork & Poultry Rub
➢ 1/8 Cup brown sugar
➢ 4 Tablespoon butter
➢ 4 Tablespoon agave
➢ 1 Bottle Sweet & Heat BBQ Sauce

**Directions:**

1. Supply your smoker with wood pellets and follow the start-up procedure. Preheat the grill, with the lid closed, to 225° F.

2. Remove membrane from back of ribs. Season with Traeger Pork & Poultry Rub on all sides. Let ribs rest for 15 to 20 minutes.

3. Place ribs on the grill, bone-side down and cook for 3 hours. While ribs are cooking, prepare the brown sugar wrap. Spread (approximately the same size as the rack of ribs) half the brown sugar, half the butter and half the agave on top of a double layer of aluminum foil. Repeat for second rack. Grill: 225 °F

4. After 3 hours, place one rack of ribs meat side down in the brown sugar, butter and agave, and wrap. Repeat with second rack. Turn grill up to 250°F and place wrapped ribs, meat side down in grill. Grill: 250 °F

5. Cook for another 1-1/2 hours and check the internal temperature. Desired temperature is 204°F to 205°F. If not at temperature, cook for an additional 30 minutes until temperature is reached. Grill: 250 °F Probe: 204 °F

6. Remove ribs from the grill and foil packet. Place unwrapped ribs back in the grill for an additional 10 minutes. Remove from grill and sauce the meat and bone side with Traeger Sweet & Heat BBQ Sauce and cook for another 10 minutes. Slice ribs and serve. Enjoy!

# Smoke-roasted Beer-braised Brats

Servings: 8
Cooking Time: 65 Minutes

**Ingredients:**

➢ 8 Wisconsin-style bratwursts
➢ low-carb beer (enough to cover the brats)
➢ 2 tbsp unsalted butter
➢ 2 large sweet onions, peeled and sliced crosswise
➢ 2 garlic cloves, peeled and smashed with a chef's knife
➢ 8 brat buns (optional)
➢ coarse ground mustard or German-style mustard

**Directions:**

1. Supply your smoker with wood pellets and follow the start-up procedure. Preheat the grill, with the lid closed, to 325° F.

2. Place the brats on the grate at a diagonal to the bars. (Don't pierce the brats or the juices will run out.) Grill until the skin is nicely browned, about 40 to 45 minutes.

3. In a Dutch oven on the stovetop over medium-high heat, bring the beer, butter, onions, and garlic to a boil. Transfer the Dutch oven to the grill.

4. Use tongs to transfer the brats to the Dutch oven and let them steep for at least 20 minutes. The brats will stay at serving temperature—160°F (71°C)—for 1 hour or more.

5. Remove the Dutch oven from the grill and serve the brats on buns (if using) with mustard.

# Egg Bacon French Toast Panini

Servings: 2

Cooking Time: 10 Minutes

## Ingredients:

- ➤ 6 Bacon Slices
- ➤ 1 Tbsp Black Pepper
- ➤ 4 Brioche Sandwich Slices, Day Old
- ➤ 2 Tbsp Butter
- ➤ 1 Tbsp Cinnamon-Sugar
- ➤ 6 Eggs
- ➤ 1 Tbsp Heavy Cream
- ➤ 1 Tbsp Maple Syrup
- ➤ 1 Tbsp Salt

## Directions:

1. Supply your smoker with wood pellets and follow the start-up procedure. Preheat the grill, with the lid open, to 375° F. If using a gas or charcoal grill, set heat to medium heat. For all other grills, preheat cast iron skillet on grill grates.

2. Place butter on griddle and spread to coat surface.

3. In a pie plate, whisk together 2 eggs, heavy cream, and maple syrup.

4. Soak both sides of bread slices in egg mixture and transfer to griddle. Cook for 2 minutes, flipping halfway until egg mixture is cooked and golden. Set aside.

5. Lay bacon on the griddle, and cook 3 minutes per side, until golden.

6. Transfer to lower right-hand corner of griddle to keep warm.

7. Crack 4 eggs on top of rendered bacon fat. Season with salt and pepper. Cook 1 minute per side, or to desired doneness.

8. Lay eggs on top of French toast, add bacon, then place the other slice of French Toast on top.

9. Transfer back to griddle for another minute to warm, sprinkle with extra cinnamon-sugar, then slice in half and serve hot.

# Scalloped Potatoes With Ham, Corn And Bacon

Servings: 4-6

Cooking Time: 60 Minutes

## Ingredients:

- ➤ 1 1/2 Cups Cooked Bacon, Chopped
- ➤ 1 Tablespoon Butter
- ➤ 1 1/2 Cup Cooked Ham, Cubed
- ➤ 5-6 Large Potatoes, Red
- ➤ Salt And Pepper
- ➤ 1 Cup Whole Kernel Corn
- ➤ Milk

## Directions:

1. Supply your smoker with wood pellets and follow the start-up procedure. Preheat the grill, with the lid open, to 350° F.

2. Smear softened butter all over the bottom of a baking dish. Slice potatoes as uniformly as possible.

3. Place enough potatoes in the pan to cover the bottom. Add some of the bacon, ham and corn on top of the potatoes. Repeat this until you've created a few layers and have used all the potatoes, ham, corn and bacon.

4. Add 1 tbsp of butter and cover with milk, till it's almost covering the mixture. Add salt and pepper to taste.

5. Place on the grill for 1 hour and enjoy!

# St. Louis–style Pork Steaks

Servings: 4
Cooking Time: 120 Minutes

**Ingredients:**

- 1 cup low-carb barbecue sauce
- ¼ cup low-carb beer or sugar-free dark-colored soda or sugar-free root beer
- 4 bone-in pork shoulder steaks, each about 1lb (450g) and at least 1 inch (2.5cm) thick
- for the rub
- 1 tbsp coarse salt
- 1 tbsp freshly ground black pepper
- 1 tbsp granulated light brown sugar or low-carb substitute
- 1 tbsp sweet or smoked paprika
- 1 tsp granulated garlic or garlic powder
- 1 tsp celery salt

**Directions:**

1. Supply your smoker with wood pellets and follow the start-up procedure. Preheat the grill, with the lid closed, to 250° F.
2. In a small bowl, combine the barbecue sauce and beer. Set aside.
3. In a small bowl, make the rub by combining the ingredients. Mix well. Season the steaks on both sides with some of the rub.
4. Place the steaks on the grate at an angle to the bars and smoke for 30 minutes. Transfer the steaks to an aluminum foil roasting pan. Pour the barbecue mixture over them. Use tongs to turn the steaks, making sure each is coated well with the sauce.
5. Tightly wrap aluminum foil over the top of the pan and place it on the grate. Braise the steaks until they're fork tender, about 1½ hours. (Protect your hands when lifting a corner of the foil because steam will escape.)
6. Remove the pan from the grill and serve the steaks immediately.

# Egg Sausage Casserole

Servings: 12
Cooking Time: 60 Minutes

**Ingredients:**

- 12 sausage links
- 30 oz hash browns, thawed
- 1 1/2 c. marble jack cheese, shredded
- 1/2 tsp pepper
- 12 large eggs
- 1 tsp salt
- 1/2 c. yellow onion, chopped
- 1 c. milk

**Directions:**

1. Supply your smoker with wood pellets and follow the start-up procedure. Preheat the grill, with the lid closed, to 350° F.
2. Grill sausage links on the preheated grill for 10-15 minutes or until heated through.
3. Remove the sausage links from grill and cut them into 1-inch pieces.
4. Spray a 9" ×13" tin pan with non-stick spray. Spread out hash browns on bottom of pan. Top with sausage pieces.
5. Combine eggs, salt, pepper, 1 c. cheese, onions, and milk in a bowl. Pour the mixture over sausage and hash browns. Then top with the remaining 1/2 c. of cheese.
6. Transfer the tin pan to the grill grate, and grill at 350 °F for 45 minutes or until the middle is set.

# Pretzel Bun With Pulled Pork

Servings: 4

Cooking Time: 300 Minutes

## Ingredients:

- ⅓ Cup Apple Cider Vinegar
- 1 ½ Cups Bbq Sauce, Divided
- 1 Qt. Chicken Stock
- ⅓ Cup Ketchup
- 3 Tbsp Pulled Pork Rub, Divided
- 1, 4 Lb. Pork Shoulder, Bone In
- 4 Pretzel Buns

## Directions:

1. Supply your smoker with wood pellets and follow the start-up procedure. Preheat the grill, with the lid open, to 400° F. If using a gas or charcoal grill, set it up for medium-high heat. In a bowl, combine the apple cider vinegar, chicken stock, ketchup, and 1 tablespoon of Pulled Pork Rub. Whisk well to combine and set aside.

2. Season the pork shoulder with the remaining 2 tablespoons of Pulled Pork Seasoning on all sides of the pork shoulder, then place on the grill and sear on all sides until golden brown, about 10 minutes.

3. Remove the pork shoulder from the grill and place in the disposable aluminum pan. Pour the sauce over the pork shoulder. It should come about 1/3 to ½ way up the side of the pork shoulder. Cover the top of the pan tightly with aluminum foil.

4. Reduce the temperature of your grill to 250°F. Place the foil pan on the grill and cook for 4 to 5 hours, or until the pork is tender and falling off the bone.

5. Remove the pork from the grill and allow to rest for 15 minutes. Drain the liquid from the pan, reserving about a cup, then shred the pork and cover with the reserved liquid. Set 3 ½ to 4 cups of pulled pork aside for sandwiches, and save the remaining for future use.

6. While pork is resting, place 1 cup of BBQ sauce in a skillet and heat to simmer. Toss in reserved shredded pork. Divide pork among 4 pretzel buns, spoon additional BBQ sauce over the top and dig in!

# VEGETABLES RECIPES

## Sicilian Stuffed Mushrooms

Servings: 6
Cooking Time: 25 Minutes

**Ingredients:**

➤ 12 Medium Fresh Mushrooms, about 1-1/2 inches in diameter
➤ 4 Ounce cream cheese, room temperature
➤ 1/4 Cup Parmesan cheese, grated
➤ 1/4 Cup shredded mozzarella cheese
➤ 8 Whole Pimento Stuffed Green Olives, chopped
➤ 3 Tablespoon Pepperoni, finely diced
➤ 1 1/2 Tablespoon Sun Dried Tomatoes, drained & minced
➤ 1/4 Teaspoon freshly ground black pepper

**Directions:**

1. Dampen a paper towel and wipe the outside of the mushrooms clean. Remove the stem. Using a small spoon, scoop out the inside of the mushroom leaving a shell.
2. Filling: In a small mixing bowl, beat together the cream cheese, Parmesan, and mozzarella. Stir in olives, pepperoni, tomatoes, basil, and pepper.
3. Mound the filling in the mushroom caps. Set each filled cap into the well of a muffin tin.
4. Supply your smoker with wood pellets and follow the start-up procedure. Preheat the grill, with the lid closed, to 350° F.
5. Arrange the muffin tin on the grill grate and bake the mushrooms for 25 to 30 minutes, or until the mushrooms are tender and the filling is beginning to brown.
6. Transfer to a serving plate or platter. Enjoy!

## Baked Breakfast Mini Quiches

Servings: 8
Cooking Time: 15 Minutes

**Ingredients:**

➤ cooking spray
➤ 1 Tablespoon extra-virgin olive oil
➤ 1/2 yellow onion, diced
➤ 3 Cup Spinach, fresh
➤ 10 eggs
➤ 4 Ounce shredded cheddar, mozzarella or Swiss cheese
➤ 1/4 Cup fresh basil
➤ 1 Teaspoon kosher salt
➤ 1/2 Teaspoon black pepper

**Directions:**

1. Spray a 12-cup muffin tin generously with cooking spray.
2. In a small skillet over medium heat, warm the oil. Add the onion and cook, stirring frequently, until softened, about 7 minutes. Add the spinach and cook until wilted, about 1 minute longer.
3. Transfer to a cutting board to cool, then chop the mixture so the spinach if broken up a little.
4. Supply your smoker with wood pellets and follow the start-up procedure. Preheat the grill, with the lid closed, to 350° F.
5. In a large bowl, whisk the eggs until frothy. Add the cooled onions and spinach, cheese, basil, 1 tsp salt and 1/2 tsp pepper. Stir to combine. Divide egg mixture evenly among the muffin cups.
6. Place tray on the grill and bake until the eggs have puffed up, are set, and are beginning to brown, about 18 to 20 minutes. Grill: 350 °F
7. Serve immediately, or allow to cool on a wire rack, then refrigerate in an air tight container for up to 4 days. Enjoy!

# Roasted Potato Poutine

Servings: 6

Cooking Time: 40 Minutes

## Ingredients:

➢ 4 Large russet potatoes
➢ Tablespoon olive oil or vegetable oil
➢ Prime Rib Rub
➢ Cup chicken or beef gravy (homemade or jarred)
➢ 1 1/2 Cup white or yellow cheddar cheese curds
➢ freshly ground black pepper
➢ 2 Tablespoon scallions

## Directions:

1. Supply your smoker with wood pellets and follow the start-up procedure. Preheat the grill, with the lid closed, to 500° F.

2. Scrub the potatoes and slice into fries, wedges or preferred shape.

3. Put potatoes into a large mixing bowl and coat with oil. Season generously with Traeger Prime Rib rub.

4. Tip the potatoes onto a rimmed baking sheet and spread in a single layer, cut sides down.

5. Roast for 20 minutes, then using a spatula, turn the potatoes to the other cut side. Continue to roast until the potatoes are tender and golden brown, about 15 to 20 minutes more.

6. While potatoes cook, warm the gravy on the stovetop or in a heat-proof saucepan on your Traeger.

7. To assemble the poutine, arrange the potatoes in a large shallow bowl or on a serving platter. Distribute the cheese curds on top. Pour the hot gravy evenly over the potatoes and cheese curds.

8. Season with black pepper and garnish with thinly sliced scallions. Serve immediately. Enjoy!

# Grilled Corn On The Cob With Parmesan And Garlic

Servings: 6

Cooking Time: 30 Minutes

## Ingredients:

➢ 4 Tablespoon butter, melted
➢ 2 Clove garlic, minced
➢ salt and pepper
➢ 8 ears fresh corn
➢ 1/2 Cup shaved Parmesan
➢ 1 Tablespoon chopped parsley

## Directions:

1. Supply your smoker with wood pellets and follow the start-up procedure. Preheat the grill, with the lid closed, to 450° F.

2. Place butter, garlic, salt and pepper in a medium bowl and mix well.

3. Peel back corn husks and remove the silk. Rub corn with half of the garlic butter mixture.

4. Close husks and place directly on the grill grate. Cook for 25 to 30 minutes, turning occasionally until corn is tender. Grill: 450 °F

5. Remove from grill, peel and discard husks. Place corn on serving tray, drizzle with remaining butter and top with Parmesan and parsley.

# Smoked Beet-pickled Eggs

Servings: 4

Cooking Time: 30 Minutes

## Ingredients:

➢ 6 Eggs, hard boiled
➢ 1 Red Beets, scrubbed and trimmed
➢ 1 Cup apple cider vinegar
➢ 1 Cup Beet, juice
➢ 1/4 Onion, Sliced
➢ 1/3 Cup granulated sugar

- ➢ 3 Cardamom
- ➢ 1 star anise

**Directions:**

1. Supply your smoker with wood pellets and follow the start-up procedure. Preheat the grill, with the lid closed, to 275° F.

2. Place the peeled hard boiled eggs directly on the grill and smoke for 30 minutes. Grill: 275 °F

3. Put the smoked eggs in a quart size glass jar with the cooked/chopped beets in the bottom.

4. In a medium sauce pan, add the vinegar, beet juice, onion, sugar, cardamom and anise.

5. Bring to a boil and cook, uncovered, until sugar has dissolved and the onions are translucent (about 5 minutes).

6. Remove from the heat and let cool for a few minutes.

7. Pour the vinegar and onions mixture over the eggs and beets in the jar, covering the eggs completely.

8. Securely close with the jar lid. Refrigerate up to a month. Enjoy!

# Grilled Ratatouille Salad

Servings: 4
Cooking Time: 25 Minutes

**Ingredients:**

- ➢ 1 Whole sweet potatoes
- ➢ 1 Whole red onion, diced
- ➢ 1 Whole zucchini
- ➢ 1 Whole Squash
- ➢ 1 Large Tomato, diced
- ➢ vegetable oil
- ➢ salt and pepper

**Directions:**

1. Supply your smoker with wood pellets and follow the start-up procedure. Preheat the grill, with the lid closed, to High heat.

2. Slice all vegetables to a ¼ inch thickness.

3. Lightly brush each vegetable with oil and season with Traeger's Veggie Shake or salt and pepper.

4. Place sweet potato, onion, zucchini, and squash on grill grate and grill for 20 minutes or until tender, turn halfway through.

5. Add tomato slices to the grill during the last 5 minutes of cooking time.

6. For presentation, alternate vegetables while layering them vertically. Enjoy!

# Roasted Pumpkin Seeds

Servings: 8
Cooking Time: 40 Minutes

**Ingredients:**

- ➢ 1 Whole Pumpkin, seeds
- ➢ olive oil or vegetable oil
- ➢ Jacobsen Salt Co. Pure Kosher Sea Salt

**Directions:**

1. As soon as possible after removing the seeds from the pumpkin, rinse pumpkin seeds under cold water in a colander and pick out the pulp and strings.

2. Place the pumpkin seeds in a single layer on an oiled baking sheet, stirring to coat. Supply your smoker with wood pellets and follow the start-up procedure. Preheat the grill, with the lid closed, to 180° F.

3. Place the baking sheet with the seeds on the grill grate, close the lid, and smoke for 20 minutes. Grill: 180 °F

4. Sprinkle your seeds with salt and turn the temperature on your grill up to 325°F. Roast the

seeds until toasted, about 20 minutes. Check and stir seeds after the first 10 minutes. Grill: 325 °F

5. Seeds will be brown because they were smoked before being roasted. Enjoy!

# Chef Curtis' Famous Chimichurri Sauce

Servings: 4
Cooking Time: 5 Minutes

**Ingredients:**

- 2 Whole lemon, halved
- 2 Medium flat-leaf Italian parsley, washed and chopped with the majority of stems cut off
- 4 Clove garlic, diced
- 1/4 Cup red wine vinegar
- 1/2 Teaspoon black pepper
- 1/4 Cup extra-virgin olive oil
- 1 Teaspoon salt

**Directions:**

1. Supply your smoker with wood pellets and follow the start-up procedure. Preheat the grill, with the lid closed, to 450° F.

2. Place lemon halves directly on the grill grate and cook for 5 minutes or until grill marks appear. Grill: 450 °F

3. Take lemons off grill and juice. Combine all of the ingredients in a food processor or blender and purée until smooth, or leave slightly chunky for some texture.

4. Add additional olive oil to taste for a milder flavor if preferred. Serve on protein or as a dip. Enjoy!

# Grilled Beer Cabbage

Servings: 4
Cooking Time: 50 Minutes

**Ingredients:**

- 2 Cabbage, head
- 1 Tablespoon extra-virgin olive oil
- 1 Teaspoon salt
- 1 Teaspoon freshly ground black pepper
- 14 Fluid Ounce Guinness Extra Stout

**Directions:**

1. Clean and core cabbages. Drizzle with olive oil and salt and pepper. Rub into the cabbage.

2. Supply your smoker with wood pellets and follow the start-up procedure. Preheat the grill, with the lid closed, to 180° F.

3. Place cabbages directly on grill grate; smoke for 15 to 20 minutes. Remove from grill and thickly slice cabbage. Grill: 180 °F

4. Place sliced cabbage in cast-iron skillet. Pour beer over cabbage and return to grill.

5. Increase temperature to 375°F and cook for 30 minutes, or until cabbage has reached desired softness. Grill: 375 °F

6. Serve with corned beef. Enjoy!

# Mashed Red Potatoes

Servings: 4
Cooking Time: 40 Minutes

**Ingredients:**

- 8 Large red potatoes
- salt
- black pepper
- 1/2 Cup heavy cream
- 1/4 Cup butter

**Directions:**

1. Supply your smoker with wood pellets and follow the start-up procedure. Preheat the grill, with the lid closed, to 180° F.

2. Slice red potatoes in half, lengthwise then cut in half again to make quarters. Season potatoes with salt and pepper.

3. Increase the heat to High and preheat. Once the grill is hot, set potatoes directly on the grill grate. Grill: 450 °F

4. Every 15 minutes flip potatoes to ensure all sides get color. Continue to do this until potatoes are fork tender.

5. When tender, mash potatoes with cream, butter, salt, and pepper to taste. Serve warm, enjoy!

# Double-smoked Cheese Potatoes

Servings: 12
Cooking Time: 35 Minutes

**Ingredients:**

➤ 4 large baking potatoes (12 to 14 ounces each—preferably organic)

➤ 1 1/2 tablespoons bacon fat or butter, melted, or extra virgin olive oil

➤ Coarse salt (sea or kosher) and freshly ground black pepper

➤ 4 strips artisanal bacon (like Nueske's), cut crosswise into 1/4-inch slivers

➤ 6 tablespoons (3/4 stick) cold unsalted butter, thinly sliced

➤ 2 scallions, trimmed, white and green parts finely chopped (about 4 tablespoons)

➤ 2 cups coarsely grated smoked or regular white cheddar cheese (about 8 ounces)

➤ 1/2 cup sour cream

➤ Spanish smoked paprika (pimentón) or sweet paprika, for sprinkling

**Directions:**

1. Supply your smoker with wood pellets and follow the start-up procedure. Preheat the grill, with the lid closed, to 400° F.Add enough wood for 1 hour of smoking as specified by the manufacturer.

2. Scrub the potatoes on all sides with a vegetable brush. Rinse well under cold running water and blot dry with paper towels. Prick each potato several times with a fork (this keeps the spud from exploding and facilitates the smoke absorption). Brush or rub the potato on all sides with the bacon fat and season generously with salt and pepper.

3. Place the potatoes on the smoker rack. Smoke until the skins are crisp and the potatoes are tender in the center (they'll be easy to pierce with a slender metal skewer), about 1 hour.

4. Meanwhile, place the bacon in a cold skillet and fry over medium heat until browned and crisp, 3 to 4 minutes. Drain off the bacon fat (save the fat for future potatoes).

5. Transfer the potatoes to a cutting board and let cool slightly. Cut each potato in half lengthwise. Using a spoon, scrape out most of the potato flesh, leaving a 1/4-inch-thick shell. (It's easier to scoop the potatoes when warm.) Cut the potato flesh into 1/2-inch dice and place in a bowl.

6. Add the bacon, 4 tablespoons of the butter, the scallions, and cheese to the potato flesh and gently stir to mix. Stir in the sour cream and salt and pepper to taste; the mixture should be highly seasoned. Stir as little and as gently as possible so as to leave some texture to the potatoes.

7. Spoon the potato mixture back into the potato shells, mounding it in the center. Top each potato half with a thin slice of the remaining butter and sprinkle with paprika. The potatoes

can be prepared up to 24 hours ahead to this stage, covered, and refrigerated.

8. Just before serving, preheat your smoker to 400 °F. Add enough wood for 30 minutes of smoking. Place the potatoes in a shallow aluminum foil pan and re-smoke them until browned and bubbling, 15 to 20 minutes.

# Baked Heirloom Tomato Tart

Servings: 4
Cooking Time: 45 Minutes

**Ingredients:**

- 1 Whole Puff Pastry Sheet
- 2 Pound heirloom tomatoes, various shapes and sizes
- 1/2 Tablespoon kosher salt
- 1/2 Cup Ricotta Cheese
- 5 Whole eggs
- 1 To Taste salt and pepper
- 1/2 Teaspoon thyme leaves
- 1/2 Teaspoon red pepper flakes
- 4 Sprig thyme

**Directions:**

1. Supply your smoker with wood pellets and follow the start-up procedure. Preheat the grill, with the lid closed, to 350° F.
2. Place the puff pastry on a parchment lined sheet tray, and make a cut ¾ of the way through the pastry, ½" from the edge.
3. Slice the tomatoes and season with salt. Place on a sheet tray lined with paper towels.
4. In a small bowl combine the ricotta, 4 of the eggs, salt, thyme leaves, red pepper flakes and black pepper. Whisk together until combined. Spread the ricotta mixture over the puff pastry, staying within ½" from the edge.

5. In a small bowl whisk the last egg. Brush the egg wash onto the exposed edges of the pastry.
6. Place the sheet tray directly on the grill grate and bake for 45 minutes, rotating half-way through. Grill: 350 °F
7. When the edges are browned and the moisture from the tomatoes has evaporated, remove from the grill and let cool 5-7 minutes before serving. Enjoy!

# Smoked Macaroni Salad

Servings: 4
Cooking Time: 20 Minutes

**Ingredients:**

- 1 Pound macaroni, uncooked
- 1/2 Small red onion, diced
- 1 green bell pepper, diced
- 1/2 Cup shredded carrot
- 1 Cup mayonnaise
- 3 Tablespoon white wine vinegar
- 2 Tablespoon sugar
- salt
- black pepper

**Directions:**

1. Bring a large stock pot of salted water to a boil over medium heat and cook pasta according to package directions. Make sure to cook to al dente, strain, and rinse under cold water.
2. Supply your smoker with wood pellets and follow the start-up procedure. Preheat the grill, with the lid closed, to 225° F.
3. Spread cooked pasta out on a sheet tray and place sheet tray directly on the grill grate. Smoke for 20 minutes, remove from heat, and transfer directly to the refrigerator to cool. Grill: 225 °F

4. While the pasta is cooling mix the dressing. Place all ingredients in a medium bowl and whisk to combine.

5. When pasta is cool combine chopped veggies, smoked pasta and dressing in a large bowl.

6. Cover with plastic wrap and place in the fridge for 20 minutes before serving. Enjoy!

## Roasted Sweet Potato Steak Fries

Servings: 4
Cooking Time: 40 Minutes

**Ingredients:**
- 3 Whole sweet potatoes
- 4 Tablespoon extra-virgin olive oil
- salt and pepper
- 2 Tablespoon fresh chopped rosemary

**Directions:**

1. Supply your smoker with wood pellets and follow the start-up procedure. Preheat the grill, with the lid closed, to 450° F.

2. Cut sweet potatoes into wedges and toss with olive oil, salt, pepper and rosemary. Spread on a parchment lined baking sheet and put in the grill. Cook for 15 minutes then flip and continue to cook until lightly browned and cooked through, about 40 to 45 minutes total. Grill: 450 °F

3. Serve with your favorite dipping sauce. Enjoy! Grill: 450 °F

## Roasted Vegetable Napoleon

Servings: 4
Cooking Time: 30 Minutes

**Ingredients:**
- 2 Whole sweet potatoes
- 2 Whole zucchini
- 2 Whole Squash
- 1 Whole red onion

- 2 Whole Bell Pepper, Red
- salt and pepper

**Directions:**

1. Supply your smoker with wood pellets and follow the start-up procedure. Preheat the grill, with the lid closed, to High heat.

2. Salt and pepper all vegetables and grill them on both sides. Begin with the peppers and onions as they will take a little longer to cook. Grill: 450 °F

## Parmesan Roasted Cauliflower

Servings: 4
Cooking Time: 40 Minutes

**Ingredients:**
- 1 Head cauliflower, cut into florets
- 1 Medium onion, sliced
- 4 Clove garlic, unpeeled
- 4 Tablespoon olive oil
- salt
- black pepper
- 1 Teaspoon fresh thyme
- 1/2 Cup Parmesan cheese, grated

**Directions:**

1. Supply your smoker with wood pellets and follow the start-up procedure. Preheat the grill, with the lid closed, to 400° F.

2. On a baking tray, mix together cauliflower, onion, thyme, garlic, olive oil, salt and pepper.

3. Place tray on preheated grill and cook until cauliflower is firm and almost tender (about 25 minutes). Grill: 400 °F

4. Sprinkle cauliflower with Parmesan cheese and continue to cook on the Traeger for another 10 to 15 minutes. Cauliflower should be tender and the Parmesan crisp. Serve immediately, enjoy!

# Roasted Fall Vegetables

Servings: 6

Cooking Time: 30 Minutes

**Ingredients:**

➤ 1/2 Pound Potatoes, new
➤ 2 Tablespoon olive oil
➤ salt and pepper
➤ 1/2 Pound Butternut Squash, diced
➤ 1/2 Pound fresh Brussels sprouts
➤ 1 Pint mushrooms, sliced

**Directions:**

1. Supply your smoker with wood pellets and follow the start-up procedure. Preheat the grill, with the lid closed, to 200° F.

2. Toss potatoes and squash with olive oil, salt and pepper and spread out on a sheet tray.

3. Place directly on the grill grate and cook for 15 minutes. Add brussels sprouts and mushrooms and toss to coat.

4. Cook another 15-20 minutes until veggies are lightly browned and cooked through.

5. Adjust seasoning as needed. Enjoy!

# Grilled Zucchini Squash Spears

Servings: 4

Cooking Time: 10 Minutes

**Ingredients:**

➤ 4 Medium zucchini
➤ 2 Tablespoon olive oil
➤ 1 Tablespoon sherry vinegar
➤ 2 thyme, leaves pulled
➤ salt and pepper

**Directions:**

1. Clean the zucchini and cut the ends off. Cut each in half lengthwise, then each half into thirds.

2. Combine remaining ingredients in a medium Ziplock bag and add the spears. Toss and mix well to coat the zucchini.

3. Supply your smoker with wood pellets and follow the start-up procedure. Preheat the grill, with the lid closed, to 350° F.

4. Remove the spears from the bag and place directly on the grill grate cut side down.

5. Cook for 3-4 minutes per side, until grill marks appear and zucchini is tender. Grill: 350 °F

6. Remove from grill and finish with more thyme leaves if desired. Enjoy!

# Baked Sweet Potatoes

Servings: 8

Cooking Time: 60 Minutes

**Ingredients:**

➤ 1 Cup butter, softened
➤ 1/4 Cup pure maple syrup
➤ 1/2 Teaspoon ground cinnamon
➤ 8 Medium sweet potatoes

**Directions:**

1. Make the Maple-Cinnamon Butter: In a mixing bowl, combine the butter, maple syrup, and cinnamon and whip with a wooden spoon. (Alternatively, blend the ingredients using a hand-held mixer or a stand mixer.) Transfer to a small bowl, cover, and chill until serving time.

2. Supply your smoker with wood pellets and follow the start-up procedure. Preheat the grill, with the lid closed, to 375° F. Arrange the sweet potatoes on the grill grate and bake until soft, 1 to 1-1/2 hours, depending on the size of the potatoes. Make a slit in the side of each, and squeeze the ends gently to fluff.

3. Serve hot with the Maple-Cinnamon Butter. Enjoy!

# Roasted Green Beans With Bacon

Servings: 4
Cooking Time: 20 Minutes

**Ingredients:**

➢ 1 1/2 Pound green beans, ends trimmed
➢ 4 Strips bacon, cut into small pieces
➢ 4 Tablespoon extra-virgin olive oil
➢ 2 Clove garlic, minced
➢ 1 Teaspoon kosher salt

**Directions:**

1. Supply your smoker with wood pellets and follow the start-up procedure. Preheat the grill, with the lid closed, to 350° F.
2. Toss all ingredients together and spread out evenly on a sheet tray.
3. Place the tray directly on the grill grate and roast until the bacon is crispy and beans are lightly browned, about 20 minutes. Enjoy! Grill: 450 °F

## Smoked Mashed Potatoes

Servings: 6
Cooking Time: 45 Minutes

**Ingredients:**

➢ 2 Pound red bliss potatoes, washed and diced medium
➢ chicken stock or water
➢ 1/2 Stick salted butter
➢ 1 Cup whole milk
➢ 1/2 Cup sour cream
➢ 1/2 Cup shredded or grated Parmesan cheese
➢ kosher salt
➢ freshly ground black pepper
➢ 1/2 Cup fresh sliced green onions

**Directions:**

1. Place the diced red potatoes into a small saucepan or stockpot and cover with chicken stock or water.
2. Bring to a boil and cook on a simmer until fork tender, then cook 4 to 5 minutes past that until soft.
3. Supply your smoker with wood pellets and follow the start-up procedure. Preheat the grill, with the lid closed, to 400° F.
4. In a separate ovenproof pan, such as a cast iron skillet, add butter and milk and place in the Traeger during start up, until melted (approximately 7 to 10 minutes). Grill: 400 °F
5. Carefully remove the butter/milk mixture from the Traeger using heatproof gloves.
6. Drain the potatoes and place into a large bowl. Add the melted butter/milk mixture and slowly mash.
7. Add sour cream, cheese and green onions, then season to taste with salt and pepper.
8. Place into the cast iron skillet, then place the skillet back into the Traeger and cook until the potatoes have a slight crust and are bubbling, about 15 minutes. Grill: 400 °F
9. Carefully remove the mashed potatoes from the Traeger using heatproof gloves. Allow to cool for 5 minutes. Scoop and enjoy!

## Roasted Tomatoes

Servings: 2
Cooking Time: 180 Minutes

**Ingredients:**

➢ 3 Large ripe tomatoes
➢ 1/2 Tablespoon kosher salt
➢ 1 Teaspoon coarse ground black pepper
➢ 1/4 Teaspoon sugar
➢ 1/4 Teaspoon thyme or basil

➢ olive oil

**Directions:**

1. Line a rimmed baking sheet with parchment paper.

2. Supply your smoker with wood pellets and follow the start-up procedure. Preheat the grill, with the lid closed, to 225° F.

3. Remove the stem end from each tomato and cut the tomatoes into 1/2 inch thick slices.

4. Combine the salt, pepper, sugar and thyme or basil in a small bowl and mix.

5. Pour olive oil into the well of a dinner plate.

6. Dip one side of each tomato slice in the olive oil and arrange on the baking sheet. Dust the tomato slices with the seasoning mixture.

7. Arrange the pan directly on the grill grate and roast the tomatoes until the juices stop running and the edges have contracted, about 3 hours. Remove from grill and enjoy!

## Braised Creamed Green Beans

Servings: 4

Cooking Time: 25 Minutes

**Ingredients:**

➢ 6 Tablespoon butter

➢ 2 Clove garlic, pressed or minced

➢ 1 shallot, thinly sliced

➢ 1 Cup heavy cream

➢ 1 Pinch ground nutmeg

➢ salt

➢ 3 Pound mixed greens such as kale, chard or collards; washed, stems removed and torn into bite sized pieces

**Directions:**

1. Supply your smoker with wood pellets and follow the start-up procedure. Preheat the grill, with the lid closed, to 325° F.

2. In a saucepan, heat 2 tablespoons of the butter over high heat until it foams. Add the garlic and shallot and cook over medium-low heat, stirring, until softened and golden, about 5 minutes.

3. Add the cream, bring to a simmer and cook until slightly thickened, about 10 minutes.

4. Add the nutmeg and salt to taste. Using a hand blender, purée until smooth.

5. In a cast iron pan, heat the remaining 4 tablespoons butter over high heat until it foams.

6. Add the greens and cook until tender but still bright green, about 5 minutes.

7. Sprinkle with salt and add the cream mixture. Cover and transfer to the grill.

8. Braise greens for 15-20 minutes until the cream is bubbling and greens are tender. Grill: 325 °F

9. Season to taste with nutmeg and salt. Serve hot. Enjoy!

## Roasted Mashed Potatoes

Servings: 8

Cooking Time: 40 Minutes

**Ingredients:**

➢ 5 Pound Yukon Gold potatoes

➢ 1 1/2 Stick butter, softened

➢ 1 1/2 Cup heavy whipping cream, room temperature

➢ kosher salt

➢ white pepper

**Directions:**

1. Supply your smoker with wood pellets and follow the start-up procedure. Preheat the grill, with the lid closed, to 300° F.

2. Peel and cut potatoes into 1/2 inch cubes. Place the potatoes in a shallow baking dish with

1/2 cup water and cover. Bake until tender, about 40 minutes. Grill: 300 ˚F

3. In a medium saucepan, combine cream and butter. Cook over medium heat until butter is melted.

4. Remove potatoes from the grill and drain water.

5. Transfer potatoes to a bowl and mash using a potato masher. Gradually add in cream and butter mixture and mix using the masher. Be careful not to overwork or the potatoes will becomes gluey. Season with salt and pepper to taste. Enjoy!

# Roasted Asparagus

Servings: 4
Cooking Time: 30 Minutes

**Ingredients:**

➢ 1 Bunch asparagus
➢ 2 Tablespoon olive oil, plus more as needed
➢ Veggie Rub

**Directions:**

1. Coat asparagus with olive oil and Veggie Rub, stirring to coat all pieces.

2. Supply your smoker with wood pellets and follow the start-up procedure. Preheat the grill, with the lid closed, to 350° F.

3. Place asparagus directly on the grill grate for 15-20 minutes.

4. Remove from grill and enjoy!

# Baked Winter Squash Au Gratin

Servings: 8
Cooking Time: 45 Minutes

**Ingredients:**

➢ 2 Cup heavy cream
➢ salt and pepper
➢ 3 Cup shredded Gruyere cheese

➢ 4 Clove garlic, diced
➢ 2 Tablespoon butter
➢ 3 yellow potatoes, peeled and cubed
➢ 1 butternut squash seeded, peeled and cubed
➢ 1 acorn squash seeded, peeled and cubed

**Directions:**

1. Supply your smoker with wood pellets and follow the start-up procedure. Preheat the grill, with the lid closed, to 375° F.

2. In a medium saucepan, cook the cream, stirring constantly, until it comes to a low boil. Add salt, pepper, garlic and shredded Gruyere cheese. Stir until cheese is melted.

3. Grease a 9x13 inch baking dish with 2 tablespoons of butter. In a large mixing bowl, combine potatoes, butternut and acorn squash. Stir in the cheese sauce. Place mixture in the prepared baking dish and place in grill.

4. Cook for 45 minutes or until potatoes and squash are fork tender. Remove from grill and let cool for 10 minutes before serving. Enjoy! Grill: 375 ˚F

# Roasted Beet & Bacon Salad

Servings: 4
Cooking Time: 45 Minutes

**Ingredients:**

➢ 2 Medium raw beets, peeled and thinly sliced
➢ 8 Slices bacon
➢ 1/4 Cup raw pecans or walnuts
➢ 2 Medium ripe pears, sliced
➢ 2 Large avocados, diced
➢ 1 Head red leaf lettuce or baby spinach, torn into bite-size pieces
➢ 1/4 Cup champagne vinaigrette

**Directions:**

1. Supply your smoker with wood pellets and follow the start-up procedure. Preheat the grill, with the lid closed, to 400° F.

2. Place beets on a foil-lined baking sheet and top with bacon. Place baking sheet directly on the grill grate (while preheating) and cook for 25 minutes. Grill: 400 °F

3. Toss to coat beets in rendered bacon fat.

4. Spread everything out in a single layer and continue to cook for another 15 minutes, or until beets are tender and bacon is crispy. Grill: 400 °F

5. Add pecans or walnuts and roast for 5 more minutes. Spoon out nuts and place on paper towels to drain and cool.

6. Once bacon is cool to the touch, roughly chop into medium pieces.

7. Place bacon, beets, nuts, pears, avocado and lettuce in a large salad bowl. Drizzle with champagne vinaigrette, toss to coat, and serve. Enjoy!

# Delicious Grilled Whole Corn

Servings: 4

Cooking Time: 25 Minutes

**Ingredients:**

➢ 3 green onions

➢ 6 Tablespoon butter, softened

➢ 1 Teaspoon chile powder

➢ 1 Teaspoon toasted sesame seeds

➢ 4 ears corn, in husk

**Directions:**

1. Supply your smoker with wood pellets and follow the start-up procedure. Preheat the grill, with the lid closed, to 325° F.

2. Place green onions directly on the grill grate and cook 15 minutes until lightly charred. Remove from grill and set aside.

3. Sesame-Chile Butter: Take butter out of fridge and let soften. Chop up charred green onions and add to butter along with chile powder and sesame seeds. Mash all ingredients together.

4. Grill corn, rotating occasionally, until husks are blackened (some will flake and fall off) and kernels are tender with some browned and charred spots, about 25 to 35 minutes. Grill: 325 °F

5. Let corn cool slightly, then shuck. Serve with the Sesame-Chile Butter. Enjoy

# Roasted New Potatoes With Compound Butter

Servings: 4

Cooking Time: 45 Minutes

**Ingredients:**

➢ 2 Pound Small Red, White or Purple Potatoes (or Combination of All Three)

➢ 3 Tablespoon olive oil

➢ salt and pepper

➢ 2 Stick Butter, unsalted

➢ 1 Tablespoon shallot, minced

➢ 3 Tablespoon Finely Chopped Herbs, Such As Tarragon, Parsley, Basil or Combination

➢ 2 Teaspoon kosher salt

**Directions:**

1. Supply your smoker with wood pellets and follow the start-up procedure. Preheat the grill, with the lid closed, to 400° F. Cut the potatoes in half and place in a large mixing bowl. Cover with the olive oil, a teaspoon of salt and generous grinding of pepper.

2. Place on a large baking sheet so there is space between the potatoes. Place on the grill and roast for 45 minutes to 1 hour, until crispy skinned. Toss once during cooking. Grill: 400 °F

3. To make the butter: Place it in a medium sized shallow mixing bowl. Use a wooden spoon or strong spatula to break it up and soften it even more. Sprinkle the shallot, herbs, and salt over the butter, then use the spoon to combine the ingredients. Taste, adding more salt or herbs if necessary. Reserve a few tablespoons of the butter to serve on the potatoes.

4. To freeze the butter for future use, place a foot long piece of plastic wrap on the counter. Spread the butter out into a 6" log across the long direction of the plastic wrap towards the bottom. Begin to roll the plastic wrap away from you to roll it into a log, twisting the sides of the plastic wrap like a candy wrapper to secure.

5. Using your hands, shape the log into an even cylinder. Once it's wrapped tightly, place in the freezer. Then when more is needed, simply slice off coins of it to serve over grilled steak, chicken, veggies, or roasted potatoes. The butter holds well in the freezer for up to one month. Enjoy! *Cook times will vary depending on set and ambient temperatures.

# Portobello Marinated Mushroom

Servings: 2

Cooking Time: 15 Minutes

**Ingredients:**
- 1 Teaspoon chopped thyme
- 1 Teaspoon rosemary, chopped
- 1 Teaspoon Oregano, chopped
- 3 Tablespoon extra-virgin olive oil
- 1 To Taste Jacobsen Salt Co. Pure Kosher Sea Salt
- 1 To Taste pepper
- 6 Whole Portobello Mushroom
- 2 Whole russet potatoes

**Directions:**
1. Supply your smoker with wood pellets and follow the start-up procedure. Preheat the grill, with the lid closed, to 450° F.

2. Mix fresh herbs, olive oil, salt, and pepper together in a bowl. Rub over mushrooms. Grill both sides of mushrooms for approximately 2-3 minutes on each side. Grill: 450 °F

3. Clean the potatoes and slice into long strips.

4. Heat the oil on the Traeger in a sauce pan; drop the potatoes in the hot oil and fry for 7-8 minutes. Let the potatoes cool slightly on a sheet pan. Enjoy! Grill: 450 °F

# POULTRY RECIPES

## Chicken Corn Fritters

Servings: 8
Cooking Time: 45 Minutes

**Ingredients:**

➢ 2 Tsp Baking Powder
➢ 1 Cup Cheddar Jack Cheese, Shredded
➢ 1 1/2 Lbs Chicken Breast, Bone-In
➢ 3/4 Cup Corn Kernels, Drained
➢ 2 Eggs
➢ 3/4 Cup Flour
➢ 1 1/2 Tsp Lemon Juice
➢ 3 Tbsp Mayonnaise
➢ Olive Oil
➢ 2 Tbsp Parsley, Chopped
➢ 2 Tsp    Champion Chicken Seasoning, Divided
➢ 1 Tbsp Scallions, Chopped
➢ 2 Tbsp Sour Cream
➢ 1 Yellow Onion, Chopped
➢ 1/3 Cup Milk

**Directions:**

1. Supply your smoker with wood pellets and follow the start-up procedure. Preheat the grill, with the lid open, to 425° F. If using a gas or charcoal grill, set it up for medium-high heat.
2. Remove skin from chicken breast. Drizzle chicken with olive oil, then season with 1 teaspoon of Champion Chicken. Place directly on grill grate, over indirect heat and grill for 25 minutes, until internal temperature is 165° F. Remove from the grill and rest for 10 minutes, then pull chicken.
3. In a mixing bowl combine onion, corn, eggs, parsley, milk, cheese, and pulled chicken.

4. In a separate mixing bowl, whisk together remaining teaspoon of Champion Chicken, flour and baking powder. Combine with the wet ingredients, then cover with plastic wrap and refrigerate for 2 hours.
5. Prepare dip: whisk together mayonnaise, sour cream, scallions, parsley, and lemon juice. Refrigerate until fritters are ready to serve.
6. Preheat griddle over medium-low flame.
7. Drizzle vegetable oil on the griddle, then add ¼ cup of fritter mixture to the griddle and cook 3 to 4 minutes per side, adding additional oil if needed.
8. Transfer fritters to a wire rack lined sheet tray. Allow to cool for 2 minutes, then serve warm with dip.

## Mandarin Chicken Breast

Servings: 4
Cooking Time: 25 Minutes

**Ingredients:**

➢ 1/2 Cup kosher salt
➢ 1/4 Cup brown sugar
➢ 1/2 Cup soy sauce
➢ 8 (6 oz) boneless, skinless chicken breasts
➢ sweet chili sauce
➢ steamed rice, for serving
➢ thinly sliced scallions, for garnish

**Directions:**

1. Pour 2 quarts water into a large mixing bowl, then add salt, brown sugar, and soy sauce. Stir until sugar and salt dissolve. Grill: 350 °F Probe: 170 °F
2. Submerge chicken breasts in the brine, cover and refrigerate for 2 hours.

3. Drain the chicken, rinse and pat dry with paper towels. Discard the brine.

4. Supply your smoker with wood pellets and follow the start-up procedure. Preheat the grill, with the lid closed, to 350° F.

5. Arrange the chicken breasts on the grill grate and cook for 25 to 30 minutes or until the internal temperature on an instant-read thermometer is 170℉. Turn chicken breasts once halfway through the cooking time. Grill: 350 ℉ Probe: 170 ℉

6. Brush chicken breasts with the sweet chili sauce during the last few minutes of cooking.

7. Remove to a platter or plates and serve with steamed rice. Sprinkle the chicken breasts with thinly sliced scallions for garnish. Enjoy!

# Turkey & Bacon Kebabs With Ranch-style Dressing

Servings: 8
Cooking Time: 25 Minutes

## Ingredients:

- 1½lb (680g) skinless turkey tenders or boneless, skinless turkey breasts, cut into 1-inch (2.5cm) chunks
- 8 strips of thick-cut bacon
- 12 fresh bay leaves (optional)
- for the dressing
- 1 cup reduced-fat mayo
- 1 cup light sour cream
- ½ cup buttermilk or whole milk, plus more
- 2 tbsp minced fresh parsley
- 2 tbsp minced fresh chives
- 1 tbsp minced fresh dill
- 2 tsp freshly squeezed lemon juice
- 1 tsp Worcestershire sauce
- 1 tsp garlic salt

- 1 tsp onion powder
- ½ tsp coarse salt, plus more
- ½ tsp freshly ground black pepper, plus more

## Directions:

1. In a large bowl, make the dressing by whisking together the mayo, sour cream, and buttermilk until smooth. Whisk in the remaining ingredients. Pour half the mixture into a small bowl. Cover and refrigerate.

2. Add the turkey to the mixture remaining in the bowl and toss to coat thoroughly. If the dressing seems too thick (dip-like), add more buttermilk 1 tablespoon at a time. Cover and refrigerate for 2 to 4 hours.

3. Supply your smoker with wood pellets and follow the start-up procedure. Preheat the grill, with the lid closed, to 375° F.

4. Place the bacon on the grate and cook until some of the fat has rendered and the bacon begins to brown, about 15 minutes. Remove the bacon from the grill to cool. Cut the bacon into 1-inch (2.5cm) squares. Set aside.

5. Drain the tenders and discard any excess dressing. Alternate threading the turkey, bacon pieces, and 3 bay leaves on a bamboo skewer. Repeat the threading with 3 more skewers.

6. Place the kebabs on the grate and grill until the turkey is cooked through, about 4 to 5 minutes per side, turning as needed.

7. Transfer the skewers to a platter. Serve with the reserved dressing.

# Grilled Whole Chicken Stuffed Sausage And Apple

Servings: 4
Cooking Time: 90 Minutes

## Ingredients:

- ¼ Tbsp Black Pepper
- 1 Tbsp Butter, Unsalted
- 1 Celery, Stalk
- ¾ Cup Chicken Broth
- ¼ Tbsp Dried Sage
- 1 ½ Cup Dry Stuffing, Unseasoned
- 1 Granny Smith Apple, Chopped
- 8 Oz. Italian Sausage, Casings Removed
- ½ Tbsp Olive Oil
- 3 Tbsp  Tennessee Apple Butter Rub
- ¼ Tbsp Salt
- ¼ White Onion, Chopped
- ½ White Onion, Sliced
- 3-4 Lb. Whole Chicken

**Directions:**

1. Supply your smoker with wood pellets and follow the start-up procedure. Preheat the grill, with the lid open, to 400° F. If using a gas or charcoal grill, set it up for medium-high heat.

2. Meanwhile, rinse chicken thoroughly and dry with paper towel. Place sliced onion in cast iron pan and set chicken on top. Place stuffing inside chicken cavity. Sprinkle Tennessee Apple Butter seasoning all over chicken and rub into skin. Tuck wings under.

3. Transfer to pellet grill and cook for 45 minutes. Add 1 cup chicken stock to pan, rotate and cook an additional 30 minutes. Remove from grill when internal temperature reaches 165° F and there is even browning. Allow chicken to rest for 15 minutes, then carve and serve.

# Smoked Turkey Legs

Servings: 4
Cooking Time: 300 Minutes

**Ingredients:**

- 1 Cup  Rub
- 1/2 Cup Morton Tender Quick Home Meat Cure
- 1/2 Cup brown sugar
- 1 Tablespoon crushed allspice berries, optional
- 1 Tablespoon grains de poivre noir entiers
- 2 bay leaves
- 2 Teaspoon liquid smoke
- 4 turkey legs

**Directions:**

1. In a large stockpot, combine one gallon of warm water, the rub, curing salt, brown sugar, allspice (if using), peppercorns, bay leaves and liquid smoke.

2. Bring to a boil over high heat to dissolve the salt granules. Cool to room temperature. Add 1/2 gallon cold water and 4 cups ice; chill in the refrigerator.

3. Add the turkey legs, making sure they're completely submerged in the brine. After 24 hours, drain the turkey legs and discard the brine.

4. Rinse the brine off the legs with cold water, then dry thoroughly with paper towels. Brush off any clinging solid spices.

5. Supply your smoker with wood pellets and follow the start-up procedure. Preheat the grill, with the lid closed, to 250° F.

6. Lay the turkey legs directly on the grill grate.

7. Smoke for 4-5 hours, or until the internal temperature reaches 165°F on an instant-read meat thermometer. Make sure the probe doesn't touch bone or you'll get a false reading. Grill: 250 °F Probe: 165 °F

8. The turkey legs should be deeply browned. Don't be alarmed if the meat under the skin is pinkish: that's a chemical reaction to the cure and the smoke.

9. Serve immediately. Enjoy!

# Chicken Parmesan Sliders With Pesto Mayonnaise

Servings: 4
Cooking Time: 30 Minutes

**Ingredients:**

- 2 Pound Chicken, ground
- 1 Cup Parmesan cheese
- 1 Tablespoon Worcestershire sauce
- black pepper
- 1 Cup mayonnaise
- 2 Tablespoon Pesto Sauce
- 3 Roma tomatoes
- 1 red onion, sliced
- Baby Spinach

**Directions:**

1. Line a baking sheet with plastic wrap. In a large mixing bowl, combine the ground chicken, the Parmesan, the Worcestershire, and a few grinds of black pepper. Wet your hands with cold water, and use them to mix the ingredients.

2. Divide the meat mixture in half, then form six 2-inch patties out of each half. Place the patties on the baking sheet, cover with another sheet of plastic wrap, and refrigerate for at least 1 hour.

3. Combine the mayonnaise and pesto in a small bowl and whisk together. Cover and refrigerate until serving time.

4. Supply your smoker with wood pellets and follow the start-up procedure. Preheat the grill, with the lid closed, to 300° F.

5. Arrange the chicken patties on the grill grate and grill, turning once, until the patties are cooked through (165F), about 30 minutes. Grill: 300 °F Probe: 165 °F

6. To serve, put a chicken patty on the bottom of a slider bun and top with a dollop of the pesto mayonnaise. Add tomato, onion, and spinach as desired. Replace the top of the bun and skewer with a frilled toothpick, if desired.

# Beer Chicken

Servings: 4
Cooking Time: 75 Minutes

**Ingredients:**

- 1 Beer, Can
- 1 Chicken, Whole
- Lemon Pepper Garlic Seasoning

**Directions:**

1. Supply your smoker with wood pellets and follow the start-up procedure. Preheat the grill, with the lid open, to 400° F.

2. Season the chicken all over with spices. Open the can of your favorite pop/beer and place the opening of the chicken over the can. Make sure that the chicken can stand upright without falling over. Place on your Grill and barbecue until the internal temperature reaching 165 degrees F (about an hour).

3. Remove from grill, slice and serve hot.

# Smoked Cheesy Chicken Quesadilla

Servings: 4-8
Cooking Time: 180 Minutes

**Ingredients:**

- 2-3 Boneless, Skinless Chicken Breasts
- 1 Jalapeno, Chopped
- 1 Onion, Chopped
- Sweet Heat Rub
- 1, Chopped Red Bell Pepper
- 1-2 Cups Salsa
- 3 Cups Shredded Cheddar Cheese

- ➢ 3 Cups Shredded Monterey Or Pepper Jack Cheese
- ➢ Taco Sauce
- ➢ 20 Taco-Size Tortilla

**Directions:**

1. Supply your smoker with wood pellets and follow the start-up procedure. Preheat the grill, with the lid closed, to 350° F. If you're using a gas or charcoal grill, set it up for medium heat. Preheat with lid closed for 10-15 minutes.

2. Sprinkle chicken breasts generously in Sweet Heat Rub and rub to coat evenly. Place chicken breasts directly on preheated grill grates and cook for 45 minutes, or until the chicken is completely cooked (165°F internal temperature), tender, and falling apart. Remove from the grill and let cool slightly. Shred with meat claws and set aside. Turn grill up to 375°F.

3. In a large bowl, add the shredded chicken, onion, red bell pepper, jalapeno, and taco sauce. Mix to combine then set aside.

4. Cut each tortilla in half. Add about 2 tablespoons each of the cheddar cheese, Monterey Jack cheese, and chicken mixture to each tortilla half. Roll the tortillas into cones, starting from the cut edge, making sure not to push the ingredients out of the tortilla.

5. Place the small bowl in the center of the pizza plan and begin to stack quesadilla cones in a ring around the bowl. The points of each cone should be in the center just touching the bowl. Sprinkle cheese over the layer and repeat another layer with the remaining cones, finishing with a final sprinkle of cheese.

6. Remove bowl from the center of the ring and place the pizza pan directly on the grill grates. Cook with the lid closed for 15-20 minutes, or until the cheese is melted and the edges are browned and crispy.

7. Fill small bowl with salsa and return to the center of the ring. Serve immediately and enjoy!

# Apple Bacon Lattice Turkey

Servings: 7
Cooking Time: 180 Minutes

**Ingredients:**
- ➢ 2 Apples
- ➢ Bacon
- ➢ 2 Celery, Stick
- ➢ (Parsley, Rosemary, Thyme) Herb Mix
- ➢ 1 Onion, Sliced
- ➢ Pepper
- ➢ Grills Champion Chicken Seasoning
- ➢ 1 Brined Turkey

**Directions:**

1. Supply your smoker with wood pellets and follow the start-up procedure. Preheat the grill, with the lid closed, to 300° F.

2. Be sure all the innards and giblets of the turkey have been removed.

3. Wash the external and internal parts of the turkey and pat the surface dry with a paper towel.

4. Slice fruit and veggies into large chunks and stuff inside turkey.

5. Liberally season the whole Turkey with Champion Chicken Seasoning.

6. Prep bacon into lattice design on a flexible cutting board. Flip onto top of turkey, covering the breasts.

7. Season with more Champion Chicken and black pepper

8. Season with more Champion Chicken and black pepper

9. Let the turkey rest for 30 minutes.

# Bbq Chicken Wings With Spicy Honey Glaze

Servings: 4

Cooking Time: 30 Minutes

**Ingredients:**

- ➤ 4 Pound chicken wings
- ➤ 6 Ounce Chicken Rub
- ➤ 2 Tablespoon corn starch
- ➤ 1 Cup honey
- ➤ 1 Cup Sriracha
- ➤ 1/2 Cup soy sauce
- ➤ 2 Tablespoon sesame oil
- ➤ 3 Tablespoon unsalted butter
- ➤ 2 Tablespoon sesame seeds

**Directions:**

1. Supply your smoker with wood pellets and follow the start-up procedure. Preheat the grill, with the lid closed, to 375° F.

2. While grill is preheating, dry off chicken wings with a paper towel. Mix the Traeger Chicken rub with the cornstarch and coat both sides of the chicken wings.

3. When the grill is heated, place the wings on the grill for 35 minutes flipping half way through. Grill: 375 °F

4. While the wings are cooking, mix the honey, Sriracha, soy sauce, sesame seed oil, and unsalted butter and heat on a stove top.

5. After the wings have cooked for 35 minutes, check the temperature. The minimum temperature must reach an internal temperature of 165 degrees F. An internal temperature between 175 to 180 degrees F may yield a better texture. Grill: 375 °F Probe: 177 °F

6. When wings are done, place in large bowl and toss with the warmed sauce.

7. Place wings on platter and sprinkle the sesame seeds. Enjoy!

# Jalapeño- & Cheese-stuffed Chicken

Servings: 4

Cooking Time: 30 Minutes

**Ingredients:**

- ➤ 4 boneless, skinless chicken breasts, each about 6 to 8oz (170 to 225g)
- ➤ 8 strips of thin-sliced bacon
- ➤ for the filling
- ➤ 4oz (110g) light cream cheese, at room temperature
- ➤ ⅓ cup shredded pepper Jack or Cheddar cheese
- ➤ 2 jalapeños, destemmed, deseeded, and minced
- ➤ 2 tbsp reduced-fat mayo
- ➤ 1 tsp chili powder
- ➤ ½ tsp coarse salt

**Directions:**

1. Supply your smoker with wood pellets and follow the start-up procedure. Preheat the grill, with the lid closed, to 375° F.

2. In a large bowl, make the filling by combining the ingredients. Mix well.

3. Use a sharp, thin-bladed knife to cut a deep pocket in the side of each chicken breast, angling the knife toward the opposite side. (Don't cut all the way through.) Spoon ¼ of the cheese filling into the pocket of each breast and gently press the edges of the pocket together to enclose. Wrap 2 slices of bacon in a spiral pattern around each breast.

4. Place the chicken on the grate at an angle to the bars. Grill until the chicken is cooked through,

the filling melts, and the bacon is golden brown, about 25 to 30 minutes.

5.  Transfer the pockets to a platter. Let rest for 2 minutes before serving.

# Chicken Breast Calzones

Servings: 4
Cooking Time: 24 Minutes

**Ingredients:**

➢  4 boneless, skinless chicken breasts, each about 6 to 8oz (170 to 225g)

➢  coarse salt

➢  freshly ground black pepper

➢  1 cup good-quality Italian tomato sauce or marinara

➢  4oz (110g) thinly sliced pepperoni or diced smoked ham

➢  4oz (110g) provolone, fontina, or mozzarella cheese

➢  8 fresh basil leaves

➢  4 thin slices of prosciutto

➢  extra virgin olive oil

➢  freshly grated Parmesan cheese

**Directions:**

1.  Supply your smoker with wood pellets and follow the start-up procedure. Preheat the grill, with the lid closed, to 425° F.

2.  Use a sharp, thin-bladed knife to cut a deep pocket in the side of each breast, angling the knife toward the opposite side. (Don't cut all the way through.) Season the inside of each breast with salt and pepper. Add a couple spoonfuls of tomato sauce to each pocket. Add 1 ounce (25g) of pepperoni, 1 ounce (25g) of provolone, and 2 basil leaves.

3.  Wrap each breast crosswise with a slice of prosciutto and then pin each breast closed with

two toothpicks. Lightly brush the breasts with olive oil and season the outside with salt and pepper.

4.  Place the breasts on the grate at an angle to the bars. Grill for 10 to 12 minutes and then turn with a thin-bladed spatula. Dust the tops with grated Parmesan. Continue to cook until the chicken is cooked through and the cheese has melted, about 10 to 12 minutes more.

5.  Transfer the chicken to a platter. Let rest for 3 minutes and then remove the toothpicks. Serve immediately.

# Lemon Parmesan Chicken Wings

Servings: 4 -8
Cooking Time: 30 Minutes

**Ingredients:**

➢  2 Tablespoons Unsalted Butter, Melted

➢  2 Lbs Chicken Wings, Trimmed And Patted Dry

➢  3 Cloves Garlic, Minced

➢  Juice Of 1 Lemon

➢  2 Tablespoons Mustard, Dijon

➢  ¼ Cup Olive Oil

➢  ¼ Cup Shredded Parmesan Cheese

➢  2 Tablespoons Parsley, Chopped

➢  2 Tablespoons Champion Chicken Seasoning

**Directions:**

1.  Supply your smoker with wood pellets and follow the start-up procedure. Preheat the grill, with the lid open, to 350° F. If you are using a charcoal or gas grill, set the temperature to medium high heat.

2.  In a large resealable bag, combine the olive oil, minced garlic, lemon zest, lemon juice, Dijon mustard, Champion Chicken Seasoning, and

chopped parsley. Seal the resealable bag and give it a good shake to mix the ingredients.

3. Once the chicken has finished marinating, remove the chicken from the marinade and drain. Place the chicken wings on the wing rack.

4. Place the wing rack on the grill and insert a temperature probe into the thickest part of one of the wings. Grill the wings for 5 minutes, then rotate, and grill for another 5-10 minutes, or until the internal temperature of the wings reaches 165°F.

5. Toss the wings in the large bowl with the melted butter and shredded Parmesan until well coated. Serve immediately.

## Smoke Roasted Chicken With Herb Butter

Servings: 4
Cooking Time: 60 Minutes

**Ingredients:**

➢ 8 Tablespoon butter, room temperature
➢ 1 Scallions, minced
➢ 1 Clove garlic, minced
➢ 2 Tablespoon Fresh Herbs (Thyme, Rosemary, Oregano, Basil, Sage or Parsley, Minced)
➢ 1 1/2 Tablespoon Chicken Rub
➢ 1/2 Tablespoon fresh lemon juice
➢ 1 (4 to 4-1/2 lb) chicken
➢ Chicken Rub

**Directions:**

1. In a small bowl, combine butter, scallions, garlic, minced fresh herbs, Traeger Chicken Rub and lemon juice. Blend well with a wooden spoon.

2. Remove any giblets from the cavity of the chicken. Wash the chicken inside and out with cold running water. Dry thoroughly with paper towels.

3. Sprinkle a generous amount of Traeger Chicken Rub into the cavity of the chicken.

4. Gently loosen the skin around the chicken breast and slide in a few tablespoons of the herb butter and cover evenly. Smear the outside of the chicken with the remaining herb butter.

5. Tuck the chicken wings behind the back. Tie the legs together with butcher's twine.

6. Sprinkle the outside of the chicken with more Traeger Chicken Rub and insert sprigs of fresh herbs into the cavity of the chicken if desired.

7. Supply your smoker with wood pellets and follow the start-up procedure. Preheat the grill, with the lid closed, to 400° F.

8. When grill is hot, place chicken directly on the grill grate, breast side up. Cook for 1 to 1-1/4 hours or until the internal temperature registers 165°F. If the chicken is browning too quickly, loosely cover the breast and legs with foil and continue to cook. Grill: 400 °F Probe: 165 °F

9. Remove from the grill and let rest 15 minutes at room temperature before carving. Serve. Enjoy!

## Sweet Cajun Wings

Servings: 4
Cooking Time: 30 Minutes

**Ingredients:**

➢ 2 Pound chicken wings
➢ Pork & Poultry Rub
➢ Cajun Shake

**Directions:**

1. Coat wings in Traeger Sweet rub and Traeger Cajun shake.

2. Supply your smoker with wood pellets and follow the start-up procedure. Preheat the grill, with the lid closed, to 350° F.

3. Cook for 30 minutes or until skin is brown and center is juicy and an instant-read thermometer reads at least 165℉. Serve, enjoy! Grill: 350 ℉ Probe: 165 ℉

# Buffalo Wings

Servings: 2-3
Cooking Time: 35 Minutes

## Ingredients:

➢ 1 pound chicken wings
➢ 1 batch Chicken Rub
➢ 1 cup Frank's Red-Hot Sauce, Buffalo wing sauce, or similar

## Directions:

1. Supply your smoker with wood pellets and follow the start-up procedure. Preheat the grill, with the lid closed, to 300℉.

2. Season the chicken wings with the rub. Using your hands, work the rub into the meat.

3. Place the wings directly on the grill grate and smoke until their internal temperature reaches 160℉.

4. Baste the wings with the sauce and continue to smoke until the wings' internal temperature reaches 170℉.

# Fried Chicken Sliders

Servings: 8
Cooking Time: 30 Minutes

## Ingredients:

➢ 8 Slider Buns
➢ ½ Cup Buttermilk
➢ 4 Horizontally Cut Chicken Breasts
➢ 2 Cups Flour, All-Purpose

➢ 1 Tablespoon Hot Sauce
➢ ¼ Cup Mayonnaise
➢ 2 Quarts Cooking Canola Or Soybean Oil
➢ ½ Cup Spicy Bread And Butter Pickle Slices
➢ ½ Tablespoon Champion Chicken Seasoning

## Directions:

1. Supply your smoker with wood pellets and follow the start-up procedure. Preheat the grill, with the lid open, to 350° F. If you're using a gas or charcoal grill, set it up for medium heat.

2. Place a deep cast iron pan on the grill and fill it with about 3 inches of cooking oil. Place a temperature probe into the oil.

3. While the oil heats, combine the buttermilk, hot sauce and Champion Chicken seasoning in a resealable plastic bag. Seal and shake to mix, then place the chicken in the bag and turn to coat.

4. Place the flour on a plate and dip the chicken in the flour to coat. Place the chicken on a wire rack set on a baking sheet and allow the coated chicken to set for 10 minutes, then dip again in the flour.

5. Once the oil in the cast iron pan reaches 350℉, place a temperature probe in a piece of chicken and fry the chicken, 2-3 pieces at a time. The oil temperature in the pan will drop by 25-30 degrees, so make sure not to put more than 3 pieces of chicken in the pan or your chicken will be greasy.

6. Fry the chicken until golden brown, crispy, and the internal temperature of the chicken is 170℉. Remove the chicken and place on a plate lined with paper towels. Allow the chicken to drain and rest for 5 minutes. Fry the remaining chicken pieces, reinserting the temperature probe.

7. Once the chicken is all fried, place the chicken on the slider buns, top with spicy bread and butter pickles, and a swoop of mayo, serve immediately.

# Injected Drunken Smoked Turkey Legs

Servings: 4
Cooking Time: 30 Minutes

**Ingredients:**
- 1 Bottle Frank's RedHot Sauce
- 1/2 Cup butter
- 1 Cup brown sugar
- 1/2 Cup whiskey or bourbon
- 3 Clove garlic, minced
- 1 Teaspoon Cajun seasoning
- 1/2 Cup chicken stock
- 6 Large turkey legs

**Directions:**
1. In a large pot, mix together all ingredients except the turkey legs. Bring to a boil. Let cool and pour the marinade into a resealable bag, then add in the turkey legs. Allow them to marinate for 24 hours in the fridge.
2. Remove the turkey legs from the bag, saving the marinade.
3. Bring half of marinade to a boil and reserve for basting.
4. Dilute the other half of marinade with chicken stock. Fill the meat injector with the marinade/chicken stock mixture and insert it into the meaty parts of the turkey leg in several places. Inject turkey legs with marinade until they plump up.
5. Supply your smoker with wood pellets and follow the start-up procedure. Preheat the grill, with the lid closed, to 250° F.
6. Place the turkey legs on the grill grate and cook for 1-1/2 to 3 hours, depending on the thickness of the legs, or until the internal temp registers 165°F on an instant-read thermometer.

Baste the legs with the reserved, boiled marinade every 45 minutes. Enjoy! Grill: 250 °F Probe: 165 °F

# Spatchcocked Turkey

Servings: 10-14
Cooking Time: 120 Minutes

**Ingredients:**
- 1 whole turkey
- 2 tablespoons olive oil
- 1 batch Chicken Rub

**Directions:**
1. Supply your smoker with wood pellets and follow the start-up procedure. Preheat the grill, with the lid closed, to 350°F.
2. To remove the turkey's backbone, place the turkey on a work surface, on its breast. Using kitchen shears, cut along one side of the turkey's backbone and then the other. Pull out the bone.
3. Once the backbone is removed, turn the turkey breast-side up and flatten it.
4. Coat the turkey with olive oil and season it on both sides with the rub. Using your hands, work the rub into the meat and skin.
5. Place the turkey directly on the grill grate, breast-side up, and cook until its internal temperature reaches 170°F.
6. Remove the turkey from the grill and let it rest for 10 minutes, before carving and serving.

# Smoked Turkey Breast

Servings: 2-4
Cooking Time: 120 Minutes

**Ingredients:**
- 1 (3-pound) turkey breast
- Salt
- Freshly ground black pepper

> 1 teaspoon garlic powder

**Directions:**

1. Supply your smoker with wood pellets and follow the start-up procedure. Preheat the grill, with the lid closed, to 180°F.

2. Season the turkey breast all over with salt, pepper, and garlic powder.

3. Place the breast directly on the grill grate and smoke for 1 hour.

4. Increase the grill's temperature to 350°F and continue to cook until the turkey's internal temperature reaches 170°F. Remove the breast from the grill and serve immediately.

# Smoke-roasted Chicken Thighs

Servings: 12-15

Cooking Time: 120 Minutes

**Ingredients:**

> 3 pounds chicken thighs
> 2 teaspoons salt
> 2 teaspoons freshly ground black pepper
> 2 teaspoons garlic powder
> 2 teaspoons onion powder
> 2 cups prepared Italian dressing

**Directions:**

1. Place the chicken thighs in a shallow dish and sprinkle with the salt, pepper, garlic powder, and onion powder, being sure to get under the skin.

2. Cover with the Italian dressing, coating all sides, and refrigerate for 1 hour.

3. Supply your smoker with wood pellets and follow the start-up procedure. Preheat, with the lid closed, to 250°F.

4. Remove the chicken thighs from the marinade and place directly on the grill, skin-side down. Discard the marinade.

5. Close the lid and roast the chicken for 1 hour 30 minutes to 2 hours, or until a meat thermometer inserted in the thickest part of the thighs reads 165°F. Do not turn the thighs during the smoking process.

# Lollipop Drumsticks

Servings: 4-6

Cooking Time: 75 Minutes

**Ingredients:**

> 1 Cup Barbecue Sauce
> 10 Tablespoons Butter, Salted
> 12 Chicken Drumsticks
> 1 Cup Hot Sauce
> Champion Chicken Seasoning
> Blue Cheese Or Ranch Dressing

**Directions:**

1. Supply your smoker with wood pellets and follow the start-up procedure. Preheat the grill, with the lid open, to 300° F.

2. Rinse chicken and pat dry with a paper towel.

3. Chop the very top of the drumstick on the larger, meaty side so the lollipops sit flatly. On the small end of the drumstick, about an inch above the knuckle, use a sharp knife or kitchen shears to cut the skin and tendons all the way down to the bone and pull the skin and cartilage off the knuckle.

4. Remove the tiny, sharp bone that sits right against the exposed chicken leg. Then, push all the meat and skin down to form the lollipop ball. Use your knife or shears to remove any excess tendons.

5. Season each lollipop generously with Champion Chicken seasoning and place in the aluminum pan with the flat side done and bones standing straight up. Then, cut 10 tablespoons of

butter into cubes of 1 tablespoon each and place evenly throughout the rows of lollipops.

6. Cook lollipop drumsticks on your   at 300°F for 1 hour; checking back every 20 minutes to baste the meat with the melted butter on the bottom of the pan.

7. For the Sauce: add your favorite bbq sauce into one aluminum loaf pan. Then, add 1 cup of hot sauce and 10 tablespoons of butter into the other aluminum loaf pan. Place them on the grill 5 minutes before your chicken is done. Stir well once it's warm and the butter has melted.

8. After 1 hour, use a thermometer to check the internal temperature of the lollipops. They will be ready to glaze when the temperature reaches 165°F.

9. Once ready, dip 6 lollipops in the bbq sauce and 6 in the buffalo sauce making sure to hold the leg and cover the meat entirely. Then, place the lollipops on the wing rack and put back on the grill for 15 more minutes or until the sauce is set.

## Whole Smoked Honey Chicken

Servings: 4
Cooking Time: 40 Minutes

**Ingredients:**

➤ 1 Tablespoon Honey
➤ 1 ½ Lemon
➤ 4 Tablespoons      Champion Chicken Seasoning
➤ 4 Tablespoons Unsalted Butter
➤ 1, 4 Pound Chicken, Giblets Removed And Patted Dry

**Directions:**

1. Supply your smoker with wood pellets and follow the start-up procedure. Preheat the grill, with the lid open, to 225° F.

2. In a small saucepan, melt together the butter and honey over low heat. Squeeze ½ lemon into the honey mixture and remove from the heat.

3. Smoke the chicken, skin side down until the chicken is lightly browned and the skin releases from the grate without ripping, about 6-8 minutes.

4. Turn the chicken over and baste with the honey butter mixture.

5. Continue to smoke the chicken, basting every 45 minutes, until the thickest part of the chicken reaches 160°F.

## Applewood-smoked Whole Turkey

Servings: 6-8
Cooking Time: 300 Minutes

**Ingredients:**

➤ 1 (10- to 12-pound) turkey, giblets removed
➤ Extra-virgin olive oil, for rubbing
➤ ¼ cup poultry seasoning
➤ 8 tablespoons (1 stick) unsalted butter, melted
➤ ½ cup apple juice
➤ 2 teaspoons dried sage
➤ 2 teaspoons dried thyme

**Directions:**

1. Supply your smoker with wood pellets and follow the  start-up procedure. Preheat, with the lid closed, to 250°F.

2. Rub the turkey with oil and season with the poultry seasoning inside and out, getting under the skin.

3. In a bowl, combine the melted butter, apple juice, sage, and thyme to use for basting.

4. Put the turkey in a roasting pan, place on the grill, close the lid, and grill for 5 to 6 hours, basting every hour, until the skin is brown and

crispy, or until a meat thermometer inserted in the thickest part of the thigh reads 165°F.

5. Let the bird rest for 15 to 20 minutes before carving.

# Delicious Smoked Turketta

Servings: 6

Cooking Time: 180 Minutes

**Ingredients:**

➢ 1 Shady Brook Farms® Turketta

**Directions:**

1. Supply your smoker with wood pellets and follow the start-up procedure. Preheat the grill, with the lid closed, to 250° F. If using a gas or charcoal grill, set it up for low, indirect heat.

2. Place the Turketta directly on the grill grate and smoke for 2½ to 3 hours, or until an internal temperature of 165°F is reached.

# Bbq Chicken Thighs

Servings: 4

Cooking Time: 35 Minutes

**Ingredients:**

➢ 6 bone-in, skin-on chicken thighs
➢ salt and ground black pepper
➢ Big Game Rub

**Directions:**

1. Supply your smoker with wood pellets and follow the start-up procedure. Preheat the grill, with the lid closed, to 350° F.

2. While grill is heating, trim excess fat and skin from chicken thighs. Season with a light layer of salt and pepper then a layer of Traeger Big Game Rub.

3. Place chicken thighs on the grill grate and cook for 35 minutes. Check internal temperature,

chicken is done at 165°F, but there is enough fat that they will stay moist at an internal temperature of 180°F and the texture is better. Grill: 350 °F Probe: 165 °F

4. Remove from the grill and let rest for 5 minutes before serving. Enjoy!

# Smoked Chicken Fajita Quesadillas

Servings: 4

Cooking Time: 45 Minutes

**Ingredients:**

➢ 2 Chicken, Boneless/Skinless
➢ 1 Tsp Chilli, Powder
➢ 1 Tsp Garlic Powder
➢ 1/2 Green Bell Pepper, Sliced
➢ 1 Cup Mexican Cheese, Shredded
➢ 1/2 Onion, Sliced
➢ 1/2 Tsp Oregano
➢ 1 Tsp Paprika, Powder
➢ 1/4 Tsp Pepper
➢ 1/2 Red Bell Peppers
➢ Salsa
➢ Sour Cream
➢ 4 Tortilla
➢ 1/2 Yellow Bell Pepper, Sliced

**Directions:**

1. Supply your smoker with wood pellets and follow the start-up procedure. Preheat the grill, with the lid open, to 350° F.

2. Combine spices in a bowl and season chicken breasts. Leave a little bit of seasoning for the vegetables.

3. Place chicken on the grates and cook for 30 minutes, flipped halfway through.

4. In a Vegetable Basket, combine all vegetables and season with the remaining spice mixture.

5. Open up the flame broiler and saute over the open flame for about 15 minutes, or until the vegetables are cooked to your liking.

6. On a tortilla, layer cheese, vegetables, sliced chicken and more cheese. Fold the tortilla and place over the open flame on your Grill. Sear until the tortilla is nicely toasted and the cheese is melted. Cut and serve with salsa and sour cream.

## Smoked Chicken Leg & Thigh Quarters

Servings: 6
Cooking Time: 120 Minutes

### Ingredients:
> 8 chicken legs (thigh and drumstick)
> 3 Tablespoon olive oil
> Pork & Poultry Rub

### Directions:
1. Place the chicken pieces in a large mixing bowl. Pour oil over the chicken to coat each piece, then season to taste with the Traeger Pork & Poultry Rub. Massage the chicken pieces to encourage the oil and seasonings get under the skin. Cover and refrigerate for at least 1 to 2 hours.

2. Supply your smoker with wood pellets and follow the start-up procedure. Preheat the grill, with the lid closed, to 180° F.

3. Remove the chicken from the refrigerator, letting any excess oil drip back into the bowl. Grill: 180 °F

4. Arrange the chicken on the grill grate and smoke for 1 hour. Increase Traeger temperature to 350°F and continue to roast the chicken until the internal temperature in the thickest part of a thigh is 165°F or the chicken is golden brown and the juices run clear, about 50 to 60 minutes. Grill: 350 °F Probe: 165 °F

5. Remove from the grill and allow the chicken to rest for 8 to 10 minutes and serve. Enjoy!

## Grilled Greek Chicken With Garlic & Lemon

Servings: 4
Cooking Time: 60 Minutes

### Ingredients:
> 2 Whole Roasting Chicken, 3.5-4lbs, each cut into 8 pieces
> 2 Whole lemons, quartered
> Cup extra-virgin olive oil
> 4 Clove garlic, minced
> 1 1/2 Tablespoon Oregano, fresh
> 1 As Needed  Chicken Rub
> 1 Cup Broth, chicken

### Directions:
1. Arrange the chicken pieces in a single layer in a large roasting pan. Squeeze the juice from each piece of lemon over the chicken, catching any seeds in your fingers. Tuck the lemon rinds in with the chicken. Drizzle the olive oil over all.

2. Sprinkle the garlic over the chicken. Dust the chicken with the fresh oregano, and season it generously with the Traeger Chicken rub, or salt and black pepper. Pour the chicken broth into the pan.

3. Supply your smoker with wood pellets and follow the start-up procedure. Preheat the grill, with the lid closed, to 350° F.

4. Roast the chicken for an hour, or until the juices run clear or the internal temperature reaches 165°F on an instant-read meat thermometer. Grill: 350 °F Probe: 165 °F

5. Transfer to a platter or plates and spoon some of the juices on top. Let rest 3 minutes before serving. Enjoy!

# Smoked Whiskey Peach Pulled Chicken

Servings: 6-8

Cooking Time: 45 Minutes

**Ingredients:**

- ➤ 3-4 pound whole chicken
- ➤ 1 cup peach juice
- ➤ 1/4 cup whiskey
- ➤ 1/4 cup melted butter
- ➤ 1/4 cup Hey Grill Hey's Sweet BBQ Rub
- ➤ 1/2 cup Whiskey Peach BBQ sauce

**Directions:**

1. Supply your smoker with wood pellets and follow the start-up procedure. Preheat the grill, with the lid closed, to 225°F, using a mild fruit wood like a peach.

2. Remove any giblets or neck from inside of the chicken and pat dry.

3. In a jar, combine the peach juice, whiskey, and melted butter. Inject this mixture into your chicken in several spots. Be sure to inject in at least 3 different places in each breast, 2 places in the thighs, and 1 time in each leg.

4. Season your chicken generously on all sides with the Sweet BBQ Rub. Place in the middle of your grill and close the lid. Smoke for 45 minutes per pound of chicken.

5. Brush liberally with the whiskey peach BBQ sauce once the internal temperature of your meat reaches 150 degrees.

6. Check the temperature in both the thighs and the breasts and when your internal temperature reads consistently 160 degrees F, remove the chicken to a rimmed serving platter or baking sheet and cover tightly with foil to allow the chicken to come up to 165 degrees F and rest for 20 minutes.

7. Shred the chicken and set it onto your serving platter. Discard the carcass or save for homemade stock. Drizzle your smoked pulled chicken with more of the Whiskey Peach Barbecue Sauce and serve on toasted buns.

# APPETIZERS AND SNACKS

## Smoked Turkey Sandwich

Servings: 1
Cooking Time: 15 Minutes

**Ingredients:**

➢ 2 slices sourdough bread
➢ 2 tablespoons butter, at room temperature
➢ 2 (1-ounce) slices Swiss cheese
➢ 4 ounces leftover Smoked Turkey
➢ 1 teaspoon garlic salt

**Directions:**

1. Supply your smoker with wood pellets and follow the start-up procedure. Preheat the grill, with the lid closed, to 375°F.
2. Coat one side of each bread slice with 1 tablespoon of butter and sprinkle the buttered sides with garlic salt.
3. Place 1 slice of cheese on each unbuttered side of the bread, and then put the turkey on the cheese.
4. Close the sandwich, buttered sides out, and place it directly on the grill grate. Cook for 5 minutes. Flip the sandwich and cook for 5 minutes more. Remove the sandwich from the grill, cut it in half, and serve.

## Smoked Cashews

Servings: 6
Cooking Time: 60 Minutes

**Ingredients:**

➢ 1 pound roasted, salted cashews

**Directions:**

1. Supply your smoker with wood pellets and follow the start-up procedure. Preheat the grill, with the lid closed, to 120°F.
2. Pour the cashews onto a rimmed baking sheet and smoke for 1 hour, stirring once about halfway through the smoking time.
3. Remove the cashews from the grill, let cool, and store in an airtight container for as long as you can resist.

## Delicious Deviled Crab Appetizer

Servings: 30
Cooking Time: 10 Minutes

**Ingredients:**

➢ Nonstick cooking spray, oil, or butter, for greasing
➢ 1 cup panko breadcrumbs, divided
➢ 1 cup canned corn, drained
➢ ½ cup chopped scallions, divided
➢ ½ red bell pepper, finely chopped
➢ 16 ounces jumbo lump crabmeat
➢ ¾ cup mayonnaise, divided
➢ 1 egg, beaten
➢ 1 teaspoon salt
➢ 1 teaspoon freshly ground black pepper
➢ 2 teaspoons cayenne pepper, divided
➢ Juice of 1 lemon

**Directions:**

1. Supply your smoker with wood pellets and follow the start-up procedure. Preheat, with the lid closed, to 425°F.
2. Spray three 12-cup mini muffin pans with cooking spray and divide ½ cup of the panko between 30 of the muffin cups, pressing into the bottoms and up the sides. (Work in batches, if

necessary, depending on the number of pans you have.)

3. In a medium bowl, combine the corn, ¼ cup of scallions, the bell pepper, crabmeat, half of the mayonnaise, the egg, salt, pepper, and 1 teaspoon of cayenne pepper.

4. Gently fold in the remaining ½ cup of breadcrumbs and divide the mixture between the prepared mini muffin cups.

5. Place the pans on the grill grate, close the lid, and smoke for 10 minutes, or until golden brown.

6. In a small bowl, combine the lemon juice and the remaining mayonnaise, scallions, and cayenne pepper to make a sauce.

7. Brush the tops of the mini crab cakes with the sauce and serve hot.

# Pig Pops (sweet-hot Bacon On A Stick)

Servings: 24

Cooking Time: 30 Minutes

## Ingredients:

➢ Nonstick cooking spray, oil, or butter, for greasing
➢ 2 pounds thick-cut bacon (24 slices)
➢ 24 metal skewers
➢ 1 cup packed light brown sugar
➢ 2 to 3 teaspoons cayenne pepper
➢ ½ cup maple syrup, divided

## Directions:

1. Supply your smoker with wood pellets and follow the start-up procedure. Preheat, with the lid closed, to 350°F.

2. Coat a disposable aluminum foil baking sheet with cooking spray, oil, or butter.

3. Thread each bacon slice onto a metal skewer and place on the prepared baking sheet.

4. In a medium bowl, stir together the brown sugar and cayenne.

5. Baste the top sides of the bacon with ¼ cup of maple syrup.

6. Sprinkle half of the brown sugar mixture over the bacon.

7. Place the baking sheet on the grill, close the lid, and smoke for 15 to 30 minutes.

8. Using tongs, flip the bacon skewers. Baste with the remaining ¼ cup of maple syrup and top with the remaining brown sugar mixture.

9. Continue smoking with the lid closed for 10 to 15 minutes, or until crispy. You can eyeball the bacon and smoke to your desired doneness, but the actual ideal internal temperature for bacon is 155°F

10. Using tongs, carefully remove the bacon skewers from the grill. Let cool completely before handling.

# Deviled Eggs With Smoked Paprika

Servings: 6

Cooking Time: 30 Minutes

## Ingredients:

➢ 6 large eggs
➢ 3 tbsp reduced-fat mayo, plus more
➢ 1 tsp Dijon or yellow mustard
➢ ½ tsp Spanish smoked paprika or regular paprika, plus more
➢ dash of hot sauce
➢ coarse salt
➢ freshly ground black pepper
➢ for garnishing
➢ small sprigs of fresh parsley, dill, tarragon, or cilantro
➢ chopped chives

- minced scallions
- Mustard Caviar
- sliced green or black olives
- celery leaves
- sliced radishes
- diced bell peppers
- sliced cherry tomatoes
- fresh or pickled jalapeños
- sliced or diced pickles
- slivers of sun-dried tomatoes
- bacon crumbles
- smoked salmon
- Hawaiian black salt
- Caviar

**Directions:**

1. Supply your smoker with wood pellets and follow the start-up procedure. Preheat the grill, with the lid closed, to 180° F.

2. On the stovetop over medium-high heat, bring a saucepan of water to a boil. (Make sure there's enough water in the saucepan to cover the eggs by 1 inch [5cm].) Use a slotted spoon to gently lower the eggs into the water. Lower the heat to maintain a simmer. Set a timer for 13 minutes.

3. Prepare an ice bath by combining ice and cold water in a large bowl. Carefully transfer the eggs to the ice bath when the timer goes off.

4. When the eggs are cool enough to handle, gently tap them all over to crack the shell. Carefully peel the eggs. Rinse under cold running water to remove any clinging bits of shell, but don't dry the eggs. (A damp surface will help the smoke adhere to the egg whites.)

5. Place the eggs on the grate and smoke until the eggs take on a light brown patina from the smoke, about 25 minutes. Transfer the eggs to a cutting board, handling them as little as possible.

6. Slice each egg in half lengthwise with a sharp knife. Wipe any yolk off the blade before slicing the next egg. Gently remove the yolks and place them in a food processor. Pulse to break up the yolks. Add the mayo, mustard, paprika, and hot sauce. Season with salt and pepper to taste. Pulse until the filling is smooth. Add additional mayo 1 teaspoon at a time if the mixture is a little dry. (It shouldn't be too loose either.)

7. Spoon the filling into each egg half or pipe it in using a small resealable plastic bag. You can also use a pastry bag fitted with a fluted tip.

8. Place the eggs on a platter and lightly dust with paprika. Accompany with one or more of the suggested garnishes.

# Chorizo Queso Fundido

Servings: 4-6
Cooking Time: 20 Minutes

**Ingredients:**

- 1 poblano chile
- 1 cup chopped queso quesadilla or queso Oaxaca
- 1 cup shredded Monterey Jack cheese
- ¼ cup milk
- 1 tablespoon all-purpose flour
- 2 (4-ounce) links Mexican chorizo sausage, casings removed
- ⅓ cup beer
- 1 tablespoon unsalted butter
- 1 small red onion, chopped
- ½ cup whole kernel corn
- 2 serrano chiles or jalapeño peppers, stemmed, seeded, and coarsely chopped
- 1 tablespoon minced garlic

- ➤ 1 tablespoon freshly squeezed lime juice
- ➤ 1 teaspoon ground cumin
- ➤ 1 teaspoon salt
- ➤ 1 teaspoon freshly ground black pepper
- ➤ 1 tablespoon chopped fresh cilantro
- ➤ 1 tablespoon chopped scallions
- ➤ Tortilla chips, for serving

## Directions:

1. Supply your smoker with wood pellets and follow the start-up procedure. Preheat, with the lid closed, to 350°F.

2. On the smoker or over medium-high heat on the stove top, place the poblano directly on the grate (or burner) to char for 1 to 2 minutes, turning as needed. Remove from heat and place in a closed-up lunch-size paper bag for 2 minutes to sweat and further loosen the skin.

3. Remove the skin and coarsely chop the poblano, removing the seeds; set aside.

4. In a bowl, combine the queso quesadilla, Monterey Jack, milk, and flour; set aside.

5. On the stove top, in a cast iron skillet over medium heat, cook and crumble the chorizo for about 2 minutes.

6. Transfer the cooked chorizo to a small, grill-safe pan and place over indirect heat on the smoker.

7. Place the cast iron skillet on the preheated grill grate. Pour in the beer and simmer for a few minutes, loosening and stirring in any remaining sausage bits from the pan.

8. Add the butter to the pan, then add the cheese mixture a little at a time, stirring constantly.

9. When the cheese is smooth, stir in the onion, corn, serrano chiles, garlic, lime juice, cuvmin,

salt, and pepper. Stir in the reserved chopped charred poblano.

10. Close the lid and smoke for 15 to 20 minutes to infuse the queso with smoke flavor and further cook the vegetables.

11. When the cheese is bubbly, top with the chorizo mixture and garnish with the cilantro and scallions.

12. Serve the chorizo queso fundido hot with tortilla chips.

# Chuckwagon Beef Jerky

Servings: 6
Cooking Time: 300 Minutes

## Ingredients:

- ➤ 2½lb (1.2kg) boneless top or bottom round steak, sirloin tip, flank steak, or venison
- ➤ 1 cup sugar-free dark-colored soda
- ➤ 1 cup cold brewed coffee
- ➤ ½ cup light soy sauce
- ➤ ¼ cup Worcestershire sauce
- ➤ 2 tbsp whiskey (optional)
- ➤ 2 tsp chili powder
- ➤ 1½ tsp garlic salt
- ➤ 1 tsp onion powder
- ➤ 1 tsp pink curing salt

## Directions:

1. Slice the meat into ¼-inch-thick (.5cm) strips, trimming off any visible fat or gristle. (Slice against the grain for more tender jerky and with the grain for chewier jerky.) Place the meat in a large resealable plastic bag.

2. In a small bowl, whisk together the soda, coffee, soy sauce, Worcestershire sauce, whiskey (if using), chili powder, garlic salt, onion powder, and curing salt (if using). Whisk until the salt dissolves. Pour the mixture over the meat and

reseal the bag. Refrigerate for 24 to 48 hours, turning the bag several times to redistribute the brine.

3. Supply your smoker with wood pellets and follow the start-up procedure. Preheat the grill, with the lid closed, to 150° F.

4. Drain the meat and discard the brine. Place the strips of meat in a single layer on paper towels and blot any excess moisture.

5. Place the meat in a single layer on the grate and smoke for 4 to 5 hours, turning once or twice. (If you're aware of hot spots on your grate, rotate the strips so they smoke evenly.) To test for doneness, bend one or two pieces in the middle. They should be dry but still somewhat pliant. Or simply eat a piece to see if it's done to your liking.

6. For the best texture, when you remove the meat from the grill, place the still-warm jerky in a resealable plastic bag and let rest for 30 minutes. (You might see condensation form on the inside of the bag, but the moisture will be reabsorbed by the meat.) Or let the meat cool completely and then store in a resealable plastic bag or covered container. The jerky will last a few days at room temperature but will last longer (up to 2 weeks) if refrigerated.

## Roasted Red Pepper Dip

Servings: 8
Cooking Time: 45 Minutes

### Ingredients:

➤ 4 red bell peppers, halved, destemmed, and deseeded
➤ 1 cup English walnuts, divided
➤ 1 small white onion, peeled and coarsely chopped
➤ 2 garlic cloves, peeled and smashed with a chef's knife
➤ ¼ cup extra virgin olive oil, plus more
➤ 1 tbsp balsamic vinegar or balsamic glaze
➤ 1 tsp honey (eliminate if using balsamic glaze)
➤ 1 tsp coarse salt, plus more
➤ 1 tsp ground cumin
➤ 1 tsp smoked paprika
➤ ½ to 1 tsp Aleppo red pepper flakes, plus more
➤ ¼ cup fresh white breadcrumbs (optional)
➤ distilled water (optional)
➤ assorted crudités or wedges of pita bread

### Directions:

1. Supply your smoker with wood pellets and follow the start-up procedure. Preheat the grill, with the lid closed, to 400° F.

2. Place the peppers skin side down on the grate and grill until the skins blister and the flesh softens, about 30 minutes. Transfer the peppers to a bowl and cover with plastic wrap. Let cool to room temperature. Remove the skins with a paring knife or your fingers. Coarsely chop or tear the peppers.

3. Place ¾ cup of walnuts in an aluminum foil roasting pan. Place the pan on the grate and toast for 10 to 15 minutes, stirring twice. Remove the pan from the grill and let the walnuts cool.

4. Place the peppers, onion, garlic, and walnuts in a food processor fitted with the chopping blade. Pulse several times. Add the olive oil, balsamic vinegar, honey, salt, cumin, paprika, and red pepper flakes. Process until the mixture is fairly smooth. Taste for seasoning, adding more salt or red pepper flakes (if desired). (If the mixture is too loose, add breadcrumbs until the texture is to

your liking. If it's too thick, add olive oil or water 1 tablespoon at a time.)

5. Transfer the dip to a serving bowl. Use the back of a spoon to make a shallow depression in the center. Top with the remaining ¼ cup of walnuts and drizzle olive oil in the depression. Serve with crudités or pita bread.

# Bayou Wings With Cajun Rémoulade

Servings: 8
Cooking Time: 40 Minutes

**Ingredients:**

➤ 16 large whole chicken wings or 32 drumettes and flats, about 3lb (1.4kg) total
➤ for the rub
➤ 1 tbsp kosher salt
➤ 1 tsp freshly ground black pepper
➤ 1 tsp paprika
➤ ½ tsp ground cayenne, plus more
➤ ½ tsp garlic powder
➤ ½ tsp celery salt
➤ ½ tsp dried thyme
➤ 2 tbsp vegetable oil
➤ for the rémoulade
➤ 1¼ cups reduced-fat mayo
➤ ¼ cup Creole-style or whole grain mustard
➤ 2 tbsp horseradish
➤ 2 tbsp pickle relish
➤ 1 tbsp freshly squeezed lemon juice
➤ 1 tsp paprika, plus more
➤ 1 tsp hot sauce, plus more
➤ 1 tsp Worcestershire sauce
➤ coarse salt
➤ for serving
➤ lemon wedges
➤ pickled okra (optional)

**Directions:**

1. Supply your smoker with wood pellets and follow the start-up procedure. Preheat the grill, with the lid closed, to 350° F.

2. If using whole wings, cut through the two joints, separating them into drumettes, flats, and wing tips. (Discard the wing tips or save them for chicken stock.) Alternatively, leave the wings whole. Place the chicken in a resealable plastic bag.

3. In a small bowl, make the rub by combining the ingredients. Mix well. Pour the rub over the wings and toss them to thoroughly coat. Refrigerate for 2 hours.

4. In a small bowl, make the Cajun rémoulade by whisking together the mayo, mustard, horseradish, pickle relish, lemon juice, paprika, hot sauce, and Worcestershire. Season with salt to taste. The mixture should be highly seasoned. Transfer to a serving bowl and lightly dust with paprika. Cover and refrigerate until ready to serve.

5. Remove the wings from the refrigerator and allow the excess marinade to drip off. Place the wings on the grate at an angle to the bars. Grill for 20 minutes and then turn. (They'll brown more evenly but will also have less of a tendency to stick.) Continue to cook until the wings are nicely browned and the meat is no longer pink at the bone, about 20 minutes more.

6. Remove the wings from the grill and pile them on a platter. Serve with the Cajun rémoulade, lemon wedges, and pickled okra (if using).

# Grilled Guacamole

Servings: 6
Cooking Time: 30 Minutes

**Ingredients:**

- 3 large avocados, halved and pitted
- 1 lime, halved
- ½ jalapeño, deseeded and deveined
- ½ small white or red onion, peeled
- 2 garlic cloves, peeled and skewered on a toothpick
- 1 tsp coarse salt, plus more
- 1½ tbsp reduced-fat mayo
- 2 tbsp chopped fresh cilantro
- 2 tbsp crumbled queso fresco (optional)
- tortilla chips

**Directions:**

1. Supply your smoker with wood pellets and follow the start-up procedure. Preheat the grill, with the lid closed, to 225° F.

2. Place the avocados, lime, jalapeño, and onion cut sides down on the grate. Use the toothpicks to balance the garlic cloves between the bars. Smoke for 30 minutes. (You want the vegetables to retain most of their rawness.)

3. Transfer everything to a cutting board. Remove the garlic cloves from the toothpick and roughly chop. Sprinkle with the salt and continue to mince the garlic until it begins to form a paste. Scrape the garlic and salt into a large bowl.

4. Scoop the avocado flesh from the peels into the bowl. Squeeze the juice of ½ lime over the avocado. Mash the avocados but leave them somewhat chunky. Finely dice the jalapeño. Dice 2 tablespoons of onion. (Reserve the remaining onion for another use.) Add the jalapeño, onion, mayo, and cilantro to the bowl. Stir gently to combine. Taste for seasoning, adding more salt, lime juice, and jalapeño as desired.

5. Transfer the guacamole to a serving bowl. Top with the queso fresco (if using). Serve with tortilla chips.

# Chicken Wings With Teriyaki Glaze

Servings: 4
Cooking Time: 50 Minutes

**Ingredients:**

- 16 large chicken wings, about 3lb (1.4kg) total
- 1 to 1½ tbsp toasted sesame oil
- for the glaze
- ½ cup light soy sauce or tamari
- ¼ cup sake or sugar-free dark-colored soda
- ¼ cup light brown sugar or low-carb substitute
- 2 tbsp mirin or 1 tbsp honey
- 1 garlic clove, peeled, minced or grated
- 2 tsp minced fresh ginger
- 1 tsp cornstarch mixed with 1 tbsp distilled water (optional)
- for serving
- 1 tbsp toasted sesame seeds
- 2 scallions, trimmed, white and green parts sliced sharply diagonally

**Directions:**

1. Supply your smoker with wood pellets and follow the start-up procedure. Preheat the grill, with the lid closed, to 350° F.

2. Place the chicken wings in a large bowl, add the sesame oil, and turn the wings to coat thoroughly.

3. Place the wings on the grate at an angle to the bars. Grill for 20 minutes and then turn. Continue to cook until the wings are nicely

browned and the meat is no longer pink at the bone, about 20 minutes more.

4. To make the glaze, in a saucepan on the stovetop over medium-high heat, combine the ingredients and bring the mixture to a boil. Reduce the glaze by 1/3, about 6 to 8 minutes. If you prefer your glaze to be glossy and thick, add the cornstarch and water mixture to the glaze and cook until it coats the back of a spoon, about 1 to 2 minutes more.

5. Transfer the wings to an aluminum foil roasting pan. Pour the glaze over them, turning to coat thoroughly. Place the pan on the grate and cook the wings until the glaze sets, about 5 to 10 minutes.

6. Transfer the wings to a platter. Scatter the sesame seeds and scallions over the top. Serve with plenty of napkins.

# Bacon Pork Pinwheels (kansas Lollipops)

Servings: 4-6
Cooking Time: 20 Minutes

**Ingredients:**

➤ 1 Whole Pork Loin, boneless
➤ To Taste salt and pepper
➤ To Taste Greek Seasoning
➤ 4 Slices bacon
➤ To Taste The Ultimate BBQ Sauce

**Directions:**

1. When ready to cook, start the smoker and set temperature to 500F. Preheat, lid closed, for 10 to 15 minutes.

2. Trim pork loin of any unwanted silver skin or fat. Using a sharp knife, cut pork loin length wise, into 4 long strips.

3. Lay pork flat, then season with salt, pepper and Cavender's Greek Seasoning.

4. Flip the pork strips over and layer bacon on unseasoned side. Begin tightly rolling the pork strips, with bacon being rolled up on the inside.

5. Secure a skewer all the way through each pork roll to secure it in place. Set the pork rolls down on grill and cook for 15 minutes.

6. Brush BBQ Sauce over the pork. Turn each skewer over, then coat the other side. Let pork cook for another 5-10 minutes, depending on thickness of your pork. Enjoy!

# Bacon-wrapped Jalapeño Poppers

Servings: 12
Cooking Time: 30 Minutes

**Ingredients:**

➤ 8 ounces cream cheese, softened
➤ ½ cup shredded Cheddar cheese
➤ ¼ cup chopped scallions
➤ 1 teaspoon chipotle chile powder or regular chili powder
➤ 1 teaspoon garlic powder
➤ 1 teaspoon salt
➤ 18 large jalapeño peppers, stemmed, seeded, and halved lengthwise
➤ 1 pound bacon (precooked works well)

**Directions:**

1. Supply your smoker with wood pellets and follow the start-up procedure. Preheat, with the lid closed, to 350°F. Line a baking sheet with aluminum foil.

2. In a small bowl, combine the cream cheese, Cheddar cheese, scallions, chipotle powder, garlic powder, and salt.

3. Stuff the jalapeño halves with the cheese mixture.

4. Cut the bacon into pieces big enough to wrap around the stuffed pepper halves.

5. Wrap the bacon around the peppers and place on the prepared baking sheet.

6. Put the baking sheet on the grill grate, close the lid, and smoke the peppers for 30 minutes, or until the cheese is melted and the bacon is cooked through and crisp.

7. Let the jalapeño poppers cool for 3 to 5 minutes. Serve warm.

# Pigs In A Blanket

Servings: 4-6
Cooking Time: 15 Minutes

**Ingredients:**
- 2 Tablespoon Poppy Seeds
- 1 Tablespoon Dried Minced Onion
- 2 Teaspoon garlic, minced
- 2 Tablespoon Sesame Seeds
- 1 Teaspoon salt
- 8 Ounce Original Crescent Dough
- 1/4 Cup Dijon mustard
- 1 Large egg, beaten

**Directions:**
1. When ready to cook, start your smoker at 350 degrees F, and preheat with lid closed, 10 to 15 minutes.

2. Mix together poppy seeds, dried minced onion, dried minced garlic, salt and sesame seeds. Set aside.

3. Cut each triangle of crescent roll dough into thirds lengthwise, making 3 small strips from each roll.

4. Brush the dough strips lightly with Dijon mustard. Put the mini hot dogs on 1 end of the dough and roll up.

5. Arrange them, seam side down, on a greased baking pan. Brush with egg wash and sprinkle with seasoning mixture.

6. Bake in smoker until golden brown, about 12 to 15 minutes.

7. Serve with mustard or dipping sauce of your choice. Enjoy!

# Cold-smoked Cheese

Servings: 6
Cooking Time: 180 Minutes

**Ingredients:**
- 2lb (1kg) well-chilled hard or semi-hard cheese, such as:
- Edam
- Gouda
- Cheddar
- Monterey Jack
- pepper Jack
- goat cheese
- fresh mozzarella
- Muenster
- aged Parmigiano-Reggiano
- Gruyère
- blue cheese

**Directions:**
1. Unwrap the cheese and remove any protective wax or coating. Cut into 4-ounce (110g) portions to increase the surface area.

2. If possible, move your smoker to a shady area. Place 1 resealable plastic bag filled with ice on top of the drip pan. This is especially important on a warm day because you want to keep the interior temperature of the grill between 70 and 90°F (21 and 32°C) or below.

3. Place a grill mat on one side of the grate. Place the cheese on the mat and allow space between each piece.

4. Fill your smoking tube or pellet maze (see Cast Iron Skillets and Grill Pans) with pellets or sawdust and light according to the manufacturer's instructions. Place the smoking tube on the grate near—but not on—the grill mat. When the tube is smoking consistently, close the grill lid.

5. Smoke the cheese for 1 to 3 hours, replacing the pellets or sawdust and ice if necessary. Monitor the temperature and make sure the cheese isn't beginning to melt. Carefully lift the mat with the cheese to a rimmed baking sheet and let the cheese cool completely before handling.

6. Package the smoked cheese in cheese storage paper or bags or vacuum-seal the cheese, labeling each. (While you can wrap the cheese tightly in plastic wrap, the cheese will spoil faster.) Let the cheese rest for at least 2 to 3 days before eating. It will be even better after 2 weeks.

# BEEF LAMB AND GAME RECIPES

## K.i.s.s Texas Bbq Style Brisket

Servings: 8
Cooking Time: 240 Minutes

**Ingredients:**

- 1 1/2 Tablespoon coarse kosher or sea salt
- 1 1/2 Tablespoon medium grind black pepper
- 2 Teaspoon chili powder
- 1 (6 lb) flat cut brisket, trimmed
- 2 Cup beer, preferably Lone Star or other Texas beer
- 1/4 Cup bacon grease, lard or melted butter
- 2 Tablespoon Worcestershire sauce
- 1 Tablespoon garlic salt
- 1 Teaspoon red pepper flakes

**Directions:**

1. Supply your smoker with wood pellets and follow the start-up procedure. Preheat the grill, with the lid closed, to 225° F.
2. Combine rub ingredients in a small bowl and stir to mix. Season the brisket generously on both sides.
3. Put a wire cooling rack in a rimmed baking sheet or other shallow pan, then place the brisket, fat-side up, on the cooling rack. Place pan and brisket on the grill grate. Grill: 225 °F
4. Combine all the ingredients for the mop sauce in a nonreactive saucepan over medium heat. Bring to a simmer and stir until the salt dissolves. Re-warm before mopping the brisket so the fat (bacon grease, lard or butter) liquefies.
5. After the first hour, mop the brisket with the mop sauce; continue to mop every hour for the first 4 hours.
6. When the internal temperature of the meat reaches 165°F, wrap the meat tightly in butcher paper. (Note: Butcher paper is more permeable, but if you don't have access to any, use foil.) Grill: 225 °F Probe: 165 °F
7. Return the meat to the grill and continue to cook until the internal temperature reaches 203°F. (Total cooking time will vary, but plan on 6 to 8 hours total.) Grill: 225 °F Probe: 203 °F
8. Transfer the wrapped meat to an insulated cooler thickly lined with newspapers or bath towels.
9. Let the meat rest for at least 30 minutes. Reserve any juices that have accumulated in the baking sheet.
10. Unwrap the brisket. Thinly slice across the grain using an electric knife or sharp carving knife. Shingle the slices of brisket on a platter and pour the pan juices on top. Enjoy!

## Ancho Pepper Rubbed Brisket

Servings: 12
Cooking Time: 720 Minutes

**Ingredients:**

- 2 ancho peppers, dried
- 1/2 cup apple cider vinegar
- 9 arbol chilies, dried
- 12 lbs beef brisket, packer cut
- 2 tsp coriander
- 1 tbsp cumin seed, whole
- 2 tsp garlic, granulated
- 1/4 cup kosher salt
- 2 tsp oregano, dried
- 2 tsp smoked paprika
- 3 cups water

**Directions:**

1. Supply your smoker with wood pellets and follow the start-up procedure. Preheat the grill, with the lid closed, to 350° F. Let it come to temperature. If using a gas or charcoal grill, set it up for medium heat.

2. Place the dried peppers in a large cast iron skillet, then transfer to the grill and cook for 5 minutes, or until fragrant and hot to the touch. Remove from the skillet, and set aside to cool.

3. Add cumin and coriander to the hot skillet, and toast for 1 minute. Remove seeds from the skillet and cool.

4. Remove stems from ancho peppers, then transfer all chilies to a food processor. Pulse a few times to get going, then process on high for 2 minutes, until coarse-ground.

5. Add in garlic, oregano, smoked paprika, and salt. Pulse 10 times to incorporate, then transfer mixture to a bowl.

6. Remove brisket from packaging, set on a cutting board, and blot dry with paper towels.

7. Use a sharp knife to trim the brisket. Start trimming with the fat side down. Trim the silver skin from the flat side, then remove the sides and corners. Remove the fat from around the point. Turn the brisket over and trim any excess fat, leaving around ¼-inch fat thickness.

8. Season the whole brisket with chili pepper rub, then set aside.

9. Fire up your  and preheat to Smoke setting. If using a gas or charcoal grill, set it up for low, indirect heat.

10. Place the brisket on the grill, then increase the temperature to 250 F, and smoke until the internal temperature reaches 165°F. After 2 hours, start spraying the brisket every 30 minutes to help retain moisture.

11. Wrap the brisket tightly in   butcher paper, then return to the grill and continue to smoke until the internal temperature reaches 200°F.

12. Remove the brisket from the gill and rest for 1 to 2 hours in an insulated cooler before slicing.

# Hot Coffee-rubbed Brisket

Servings: 8
Cooking Time: 240 Minutes

**Ingredients:**

- aluminum foil
- 12 lbs beef brisket, packer cut
- java chop house rub

**Directions:**

1. Inject the brisket with 1 cup of beef broth, being sure to inject with the grain, spacing 1 inch apart.

2. Season the whole brisket with Java Chophouse, then set aside.

3. Supply your smoker with wood pellets and follow the start-up procedure. Preheat the grill, with the lid closed, to 350° F. If using a gas or charcoal grill, set it up for medium heat.

4. Place the brisket, directly on the grill grate, fat side down, and cook for 1 hour. Begin spraying with broth (1 cup total) every 15 minutes until the internal temperature reaches 160 to 165° F (about 30 to 60 min).

5. Remove brisket from the grill and set on a foil-lined tray. Bring up the sides of the foil, then slowly pour the remaining cup of broth over the top of the brisket, giving time to allow broth to seep into the brisket. Wrap with foil, then set on a sheet tray and return to the grill.

6. Reduce temperature to 275°F and cook for an additional 1 ½ to 2 1/2 hours.

7. Begin checking the brisket for tenderness after 1 hour. Punch thermometer probe or skewer into brisket. Desired tenderness is achieved when the probe or skewer easily slides into the brisket, like butter. If the brisket is slightly tough, repeat this test every 30 minutes. The target temperature is between 206 and 210° F.

8. Remove the brisket from the grill, and cut foil to vent. Allow the brisket to rest for 30 to 45 minutes before slicing. Separate the point from the flat. Slice the flat against the grain, then cube the brisket point for burnt ends. Serve warm.

## Citrus Grilled Lamb Chops

Servings: 4 - 6
Cooking Time: 15 Minutes

**Ingredients:**

➢ 2 Tablespoons Chophouse Steak Seasoning
➢ 4 Finely Garlic Clove, Minced
➢ 2 Pounds Thick Cut Rib Chops Or Lamb Loin
➢ Juice From 1/2 Lemon
➢ Juice From 1/2 Lime
➢ ¼ Cup Olive Oil
➢ 3 Tablespoons Orange Juice
➢ ¼ Cup Red Wine Vinegar

**Directions:**

1. In a mixing bowl, whisk together all the ingredients and 2 tbsp Chophouse Steak. Place the lamb chops in a glass baking pan and pour the marinade over the top. Flip the chops over a few times to make sure that they are completely coated.

2. Cover the glass pan in aluminum foil and allow the lamb chops to marinade for 4-12 hours.

Once the meat has finished marinating, drain off the excess marinade and discard.

3. Supply your smoker with wood pellets and follow the start-up procedure. Preheat the grill, with the lid closed, to 400° F. If you're using a gas or charcoal grill, set it up for medium high heat. Grill the chops for 5-7 minutes per side, then lower the temperature to 350°F or medium heat, and flip and grill for another 5-7 minutes.

4. Remove the lamb chops from the grill, cover in foil, and allow to rest for 5 minutes before serving.

## Slow Smoked Rib-eye Roast

Servings: 6
Cooking Time: 240 Minutes

**Ingredients:**

➢ 1 (4-6 lb) rib-eye roast
➢ 4 Tablespoon yellow mustard
➢ 1 Tablespoon Worcestershire sauce
➢ 1 Clove garlic, minced
➢ Prime Rib Rub
➢ 4 Sprig fresh thyme

**Directions:**

1. Supply your smoker with wood pellets and follow the start-up procedure. Preheat the grill, with the lid closed, to 250° F.

2. While the Traeger is warming up, prepare roast. Trim excess fat from the top of the roast down to 1/4 inch thick.

3. In a small bowl, combine the mustard, Worcestershire sauce and garlic. Cover entire roast with the mustard mixture and season liberally with Traeger Prime Rib rub.

4. Lay the sprigs of fresh thyme on the top of the roast.

5. Place the roast directly on the grill grate and smoke until the internal temperature of the roast reaches 135°F for rare or 145°F for medium, about 3 to 4 hours. Grill: 250 °F Probe: 135 °F

6. Remove roast from grill. Tent with foil and rest for 20 minutes before carving. Enjoy!

# Grilled Double Burgers With Texas Spicy Bbq Sauce

Servings: 4

Cooking Time: 30 Minutes

## Ingredients:

➢ 3 Pound ground beef
➢ 4 Tablespoon Beef Rub
➢ 1/2 Pound bacon
➢ 8 Slices cheddar cheese
➢ 4 Whole burger buns, for serving
➢ 1 Cup Texas Spicy BBQ Sauce
➢ sliced pickles, for serving

## Directions:

1. Form ground beef into eight 1/3 pound patties. Season each patty on both sides with Traeger Beef Rub.

2. Supply your smoker with wood pellets and follow the start-up procedure. Preheat the grill, with the lid closed, to 350° F.

3. For the Bacon: Place bacon slices directly on grill grate and cook for 15 to 20 minutes, or until crispy. Grill: 350 °F

4. Increase the Traeger temperature to 450°F and preheat. Grill: 450 °F

5. Place burger patties directly on grill grate and cook for 4 minutes on each side, or to desired doneness. Grill: 450 °F

6. Top each patty with a slice of cheddar cheese and cook, lid closed, until cheese melts.

7. To serve, spread the Traeger Texas Spicy BBQ Sauce onto each bottom bun and top with the pickles and patty, then repeat with BBQ sauce, pickles, patty, BBQ sauce, and finally the bacon. Top with top bun. Enjoy!

# Mustard Garlic Crusted Prime Rib

Servings: 8

Cooking Time: 195 Minutes

## Ingredients:

➢ 1 (3 Rib) Beef, Prime Rib Roast
➢ 1 Tbsp Black Pepper
➢ 2 Tbsp Garlic, Crushed
➢ 1 Cup Mustard, Whole Grain
➢ 2 Tbsp Salt, Kosher

## Directions:

1. Supply your smoker with wood pellets and follow the start-up procedure. Preheat the grill, with the lid closed, to 450° F.

2. Combine salt, black pepper, mustard and garlic in a bowl. Evenly rub the seasoning all over coating the entire surface of the roast.

3. Once your grill is preheated, place the roast on the grates, ensuring the ribs are facing the back end of the grill. Once the roast is placed on the grill, shut the lid to the grill.

4. After 45 minutes, lower the temperature of the grill to 325°F. Cook for an additional 2.5 hours or until the internal temperature reaches 125°F. Remove the roast, letting it rest for about 15 minutes. Slice and enjoy!

# Flank Steak Breakfast Potato Burrito

Servings: 4
Cooking Time: 30 Minutes

**Ingredients:**

- 2 avocado
- 1 cup bacon slices, diced
- 2 tbsp butter
- 1 cup cheddar cheese, shredded
- 2 lbs flank steak
- 4 large flour tortillas
- tt hot sauce
- 2 tsp olive oil
- 1/2 cup onion, chopped
- chop house steak rub
- 2 cups potatoes, diced

**Directions:**

1. Supply your smoker with wood pellets and follow the start-up procedure. Preheat the grill, with the lid closed, to 425° F. If using a gas or charcoal grill, set it up for medium-high heat. Preheat griddle to medium-low flame.

2. Drizzle olive oil over steak, then generously season steak with the Chop House Steak Rub. Grill steak 3 minutes [depending on thickness of steak] per side for medium-rare. Remove steak from grill and allow the steak to rest for 10 minutes, then thinly slice against the grain. Set aside.

3. Turn off the grill, then place tortillas inside to warm.

4. Add bacon to the griddle and cook for 2 minutes, then add potatoes to bacon and cook for 2 minutes. Add onions, then cook mixture until bacon is crisp, potatoes have browned, and onions are translucent. Set mixture aside.

5. Melt butter on griddle and then cook scrambled eggs. Set aside.

6. To assemble breakfast burritos, sprinkle cheddar cheese on tortillas. Add scrambled egg, sliced steak, potatoes, and sprinkle with more cheese. Wrap tortillas, by folding sides in, then rolling from the bottom up.

7. Serve hot with fresh avocado and hot sauce.

# Burnt Beer Beef Brisket

Servings: 10-12
Cooking Time: 1440 Minutes

**Ingredients:**

- 1 Cup Apple Cider Vinegar
- 1 Jar Barbecue Sauce
- 1/2 (Any Brand) Beer, Can
- Beef And Brisket Rub
- 10 - 12 Pound Whole Beef Brisket
- 2 Tablespoons Worcestershire Sauce

**Directions:**

1. Remove the brisket from the refrigerator. Trimming a cold brisket is easier than trimming a room temperature brisket. Flip the brisket over so that the pointed end of the meat is facing under. Cut away any silver skin or excess fat from the flat muscle and discard. Next, there will be a large, crescent shaped fat section on the flat of the meat. Trim that fat until it is smooth against the meat so that it looks like a seamless transition between the point and flat. Flip the brisket over and trim the fat cap to ¼ inch thick.

2. Generously season the trimmed brisket on all sides with the Beef and Brisket Seasoning.

3. In a bowl, mix together the beer (for a gluten free brisket, be sure to use GF beer), apple cider vinegar and Worcestershire sauce to make mop sauce.

4. Supply your smoker with wood pellets and follow the start-up procedure. Preheat the grill, with the lid closed, to 225° F. Place the brisket in the smoker, insert a temperature probe, and smoke until the internal temperature reads 165°F, about 8 hours. Baste the brisket with the mop sauce every 2 hours to keep it moist. Once the brisket reaches 165°F, remove from the smoker, wrap in butcher paper, folding the edges over to form a leak proof seal, and return to the smoker seam-side down for another 5-8 hours, or until the brisket reaches 202°F.

5. Remove from the smoker, place in an insulated cooler, and allow to rest for 3 hours. Once the brisket has finished resting, heat your smoker to 275°F. Unwrap the brisket and cut the flat from the point. Re wrap the flat and save for another recipe. Cut the point into chunks, coat in barbecue sauce, and sprinkle with Beef and Brisket seasoning.

6. Smoke the burnt ends for 1 hour, or until deeply burnished and glazed. Serve and enjoy!

# Smoked Garlic Meatloaf

Servings: 8
Cooking Time: 180 Minutes

**Ingredients:**
- 2 Tsp Apple Cider Vinegar
- 2 Lbs Beef, Ground
- 1/2 Tsp Chipotle Pepper Flakes
- 3 Cups Crushed Chips Corn Tortillas
- 2 Grated Garlic, Cloves
- 2/3 Cup Ketchup
- 1 Small Grated Onion, Chopped
- 4 Oz Into Sticks Pepper Jack Cheese, Sliced
- 2 Tbsp Competition Smoked Rub
- 1 Lbs Pork, Ground

- 1/4 Cup Tomato Paste
- 1 Tsp Worcestershire Sauce

**Directions:**
1. Supply your smoker with wood pellets and follow the start-up procedure. Preheat the grill, with the lid closed, to 250° F.
2. First make the glaze: in a bowl, combine the ketchup, tomato paste, vinegar, Worcestershire, chipotle flakes and Competition Smoked Seasoning. Whisk well to combine and set aside.
3. In a large bowl, mix together the crushed corn chips, eggs, onion and garlic. Add 2/3rds of the glaze to this mixture, reserving the rest for glazing the meatloaf. Mix well to combine and allow to sit until the corn chips have hydrated.
4. Add the ground beef and pork to the corn chip mixture and mix until everything is well distributed.
5. Form the meatloaf into a log and push the sticks of pepper jack cheese into the center of the meatloaf and cover with the meat mixture. Loosely wrap in tin foil and poke holes in the foil with a knife to allow smoke to penetrate.
6. Grill for 1 ½ hours covered, then remove the top half of the tin foil, glaze with reserved glaze, and grill for another 1 ½ hours or until the internal temperature is 165F.

# Smoked Seed Pastrami

Servings: 16
Cooking Time: 480 Minutes

**Ingredients:**
- For the brisket and brine:
- 1 beef brisket flat with plenty of fat intact (6 to 8 pounds)
- 2 quarts hot water and 2 quarts ice water
- 2/3 cup coarse salt (sea or kosher)

- ➢ 2 teaspoons pink curing salt (Prague Powder No. 1 or Insta Cure No. 1)
- ➢ 1 small onion, peeled and cut in half widthwise
- ➢ 8 cloves garlic, peeled and cut in half widthwise
- ➢ For the spice rub:
- ➢ 1/2 cup cracked black peppercorns
- ➢ 1/2 cup coriander seeds
- ➢ 2 tablespoons mustard seeds
- ➢ 1 tablespoon light or dark brown sugar
- ➢ 1 teaspoon ground ginger
- ➢ Beer (optional)

**Directions:**

1. Trim the brisket, leaving a fat cap on top at least 1/4 inch thick.

2. Make the brine: Place the hot water, coarse salt, and pink salt in a large bowl or plastic tub and whisk until the salt crystals are dissolved. Stir in the ice water, onion, and garlic. Place the brisket in a jumbo heavy-duty resealable plastic bag. Add the brine and seal the top, squeezing out the air as you go. Place in a second bag and seal, then place in an aluminum foil pan or roasting pan to contain any leaks. Brine the brisket in the refrigerator for 12 days, turning it over once a day.

3. Make the rub: Place the peppercorns, coriander seeds, mustard seeds, brown sugar, and ginger in a spice mill and grind to a coarse powder, running the machine in short bursts, working in batches as needed. The final rub should feel gritty like coarse sand.

4. Drain the brisket, rinse well under cold running water, and blot dry with paper towels. Place it on a rimmed baking sheet or in a roasting pan and thickly crust it on all sides with the rub.

5. Supply your smoker with wood pellets and follow the start-up procedure. Preheat the grill, with the lid closed, to 225 °F-250 °F. Fill an aluminum foil pan with water or beer to a depth of 3 inches and place it below the rack on which you'll be smoking the ribs.

6. Place the pastrami fat side up in the smoker, directly on the rack. Smoke the pastrami until crusty and black on the outside and cooked to 175 °F on an instant-read thermometer, 7 to 8 hours.

7. Wrap the pastrami in butcher paper. Return it to the smoker. Continue cooking until the internal temperature is 200 °F and the meat is tender enough to pierce with a gloved finger or wooden spoon handle, an additional 1 to 2 hours, or as needed. (You'll need to unwrap it to check it.)

8. Transfer the wrapped pastrami to an insulated cooler and let rest for 1 to 2 hours. Unwrap and slice crosswise (across the grain) for serving.

## Carrot Elk Burgers

Servings: 4
Cooking Time: 15 Minutes

**Ingredients:**

- ➢ To Taste, Blackened Sriracha Rub Seasoning
- ➢ 1/2 Tbsp Butter
- ➢ To Taste, Cilantro Mayonnaise
- ➢ 4 Pieces Green Leaf Lettuce
- ➢ 2 Lbs Ground Elk
- ➢ 4 Hamburger Buns
- ➢ 1 Jalepeno, Sliced
- ➢ 4 Pickled Carrots

**Directions:**

1. Place ground elk in a mixing bowl and season with Blackened Sriracha. Divide into 4 portions, then form into large patties.

2. Supply your smoker with wood pellets and follow the start-up procedure. Preheat the grill, with the lid open, to medium heat. If using a gas or charcoal grill, set it up for medium heat and use a cast iron skillet.

3. Place butter on the left side of the griddle and let melt. Place buns on the left side (on melted butter), and burger patties on the right side.

4. Toast the buns, then turn off the burner, keeping the buns in place to keep warm. Cook the burgers 2 to 3 minutes per side, then remove from the griddle and allow to rest for 5 minutes.

5. Assemble burger: bottom bun, cilantro mayonnaise, lettuce, burger, pickled carrots, sliced jalapeño, cilantro mayonnaise on top bun.

# Leftover Tri Tip Sandwich

Servings: 4
Cooking Time: 10 Minutes

**Ingredients:**

➤ 4 Slices Cooked And Sliced In Half Bacon
➤ 4 Cheddar Cheese, Slices
➤ 4 Eggs
➤ 4 Split And Toasted English Muffins
➤ 1 Cup Cook Thinly Sliced Tri-Tip Roast

**Directions:**

1. Supply your smoker with wood pellets and follow the start-up procedure. Preheat the grill, with the lid closed, to 350° F.

2. In a heavy saucepan, bring water to a bare simmer. Using a spoon, stir the water to form a whirlpool and crack an egg into the water. Poach the egg for 5-7 minutes, or until the white is set but the yolk is still runny. Repeat with the remaining eggs.

3. Assemble the sandwiches: top each sandwich with a slice of cheddar cheese, two halves of a bacon slice, tri-tip, and a poached egg.

4. Grill for 5 minutes, or until everything is warmed through and the cheese is melted. Serve immediately.

# Italian Meatballs

Servings: 6
Cooking Time: 90 Minutes

**Ingredients:**

➤ 1lb (450g) ground beef (85/15), well chilled
➤ ½lb (225g) Italian sausage, well chilled
➤ 1 large egg, beaten
➤ ½ cup finely grated Parmesan, Asiago, or Romano cheese
➤ ½ cup panko or other breadcrumbs
➤ 1 tsp Italian seasoning
➤ 1 tsp coarse salt
➤ ½ tsp freshly ground black pepper
➤ 1lb (450g) thin-sliced bacon, halved crosswise
➤ low-carb barbecue sauce, (optional)

**Directions:**

1. Supply your smoker with wood pellets and follow the start-up procedure. Preheat the grill, with the lid closed, to 250° F.

2. Place the ground beef, Italian sausage, egg, cheese, breadcrumbs, Italian seasoning, and salt and pepper in a large bowl. Wet your hands with cold water. Form your hands into claw shapes and combine the ingredients using a light touch.

3. Form the mixture into 24 equal-sized balls. Wrap each with a half strip of bacon and secure the ends with a toothpick.

4. Place the meatballs on the grate and smoke until the bacon has rendered its fat and the internal temperature reaches 160°F (71°C), about 1 to 1½ hours. Brush the meatballs with barbecue sauce (if using) during the last 10 minutes of smoking.

5. Transfer the meatballs to a platter. Let rest for 5 minutes before serving.

## Smoked Bacon Brisket Flat

Servings: 4
Cooking Time: 480 Minutes

**Ingredients:**
- 1/2 lbs bacon
- 4 lbs brisket flat, trimmed
- tt lonestar brisket rub

**Directions:**
1. Supply your smoker with wood pellets and follow the start-up procedure. Preheat the grill, with the lid open, to 250° F. If using a gas or charcoal grill, set it up for low, indirect heat.

2. Place the brisket in a foil-lined aluminum pan. Season the fat side of the brisket with Lonestar Brisket Rub, then flip and season the meat side with additional rub.

3. Transfer the brisket to the grill and smoke for 1 hour.

4. Use tongs to flip the brisket over, so the fat side is up, then drape half the bacon slices over the brisket. Smoke for 2 hours, then remove the browned bacon, and set aside.

5. Lay the remaining raw bacon strips over the brisket, and continue cooking until these new bacon strips are browned and the internal temperature of the brisket reads 202°F, which will likely take an additional 3 to 4 hours cook time.

6. Remove the brisket from the grill, and rest for 1 hour, then slice thin. Serve warm.

## Baked Venison Tater Tot Casserole

Servings: 4
Cooking Time: 40 Minutes

**Ingredients:**
- 2 Pound Venison, ground
- 2 Can Peas, canned
- 2 Can cream of mushroom soup
- 28 Ounce frozen tater tots

**Directions:**
1. Cook ground venison in a medium sauté pan over medium high until browned. Drain off excess fat and set venison aside.

2. In a 13x9 pan, combine venison, peas and soup. Top with tater tots.

3. Supply your smoker with wood pellets and follow the start-up procedure. Preheat the grill, with the lid closed, to 350° F.

4. Place casserole dish directly on grill grate and cook for 30 minutes. Serve hot, enjoy!

## Smoked Peppered Beef Tenderloin

Servings: 4
Cooking Time: 60 Minutes

**Ingredients:**
- 1 (2 to 2-1/2 lb) Snake River Farms Beef Tenderloin Roast, trimmed
- 1/2 Cup Dijon mustard
- 2 Clove garlic, minced to a paste
- 2 Tablespoon bourbon or strong cold coffee
- Jacobsen Salt Co. Pure Kosher Sea Salt
- coarse ground black and green peppercorns

**Directions:**

1. Lay the tenderloin on a large piece of plastic wrap.

2. Combine the mustard, garlic and bourbon in a small bowl. Slather the mixture evenly all over the tenderloin. Wrap in plastic and allow to sit at room temperature for 1 hour.

3. Unwrap the plastic wrap and generously season the tenderloin on all sides with the salt and ground black and green peppercorns.

4. Supply your smoker with wood pellets and follow the start-up procedure. Preheat the grill, with the lid closed, to 180° F.

5. Place the tenderloin directly on the grill grate and smoke for 60 minutes. Grill: 180 °F

6. Remove the tenderloin from the grill and set aside. Increase the grill temperature to 400°F. Once the grill is hot, place the tenderloin back on the grill. Roast until the internal temperature reaches 130°F, about 20 to 30 minutes depending on the thickness of the tenderloin. Do not overcook. Grill: 400 °F Probe: 130 °F

7. Let rest for 10 minutes before slicing. Enjoy!

# Jalapeño Beef Jerky

Servings: 8
Cooking Time: 240 Minutes

**Ingredients:**

➢ 2 jalapeños, stemmed and seeded (or leave seeds in for a hotter jerky)
➢ 1/4 Cup lime juice
➢ 1/4 Cup soy sauce
➢ 4 Tablespoon brown sugar
➢ 1 Cup Mexican beer
➢ 2 Tablespoon Morton Tender Quick Home Meat Cure

➢ 2 Pound beef top or bottom round, sirloin tip, flank steak or wild game

**Directions:**

1. In a blender or small food processor, combine the jalapeños, lime juice, soy sauce, curing salt and brown sugar and process until the jalapeño is finely chopped. Set aside.

2. With a sharp knife, trim any fat or connective tissue from the meat. Slice the beef into 1/4 inch thick slices against the grain. (This is easier if the meat is partially frozen.)

3. Place the beef slices in a large resealable bag. Transfer jalapeño mixture to the resealable bag and top with beer. Massage the bag so that all the slices get coated with the marinade. Seal and refrigerate for several hours, or overnight.

4. Supply your smoker with wood pellets and follow the start-up procedure. Preheat the grill, with the lid closed, to 180° F.

5. Remove the beef from the marinade and discard the marinade. Dry the beef slices between paper towels. Arrange the meat in a single layer directly on the grill grate. Grill: 180 °F

6. Smoke for 4 to 5 hours, or until the jerky is dry but still chewy and somewhat pliant when you bend a piece. Grill: 180 °F

7. Transfer to a cooling rack and rest for an hour at room temperature.

8. Store in a resealable bag. Squeeze any air from the bag, and refrigerate the jerky. It will keep for several weeks in the fridge.

# Beef Brisket With Chophouse Steak Rub

Servings: 12
Cooking Time: 480 Minutes

**Ingredients:**
- As Needed, Chop House Steak Rub
- 1, 10 To 12 Lb Whole Beef Brisket

**Directions:**
1. Supply your smoker with wood pellets and follow the start-up procedure. Preheat the grill, with the lid closed, to 250° F.
2. While the grill is heating up, trim your brisket of excess fat, score the meat against the grain and season with Chop House Steak Rub or your favorite seasoning.
3. Place your brisket on the grates, fat side up and cook for 7-8 hours or until the internal temperature reaches 190°F. If the meat is not probe tender, keep cooking until your temperature probe can easily slide into the meat with little to no resistance.
4. Remove from the grill and allow to rest for 20-30 minutes.
5. Slice against the grain and enjoy!

# Grilled Bacon-wrapped Hot Dogs

Servings: 8
Cooking Time: 20 Minutes

**Ingredients:**
- 12 Whole hot dogs
- 8 Ounce Cheese, Colby/Cheddar
- 12 Bacon, sliced
- 12 hot dog buns

**Directions:**

1. Slice the cheese into 8 long strips. Slice the hot dogs lengthwise, leaving a "hinge" on one side, and tuck a piece of cheese into each.
2. Wrap a slice of bacon in a spiral fashion around each hot dog and secure with toothpicks.
3. Supply your smoker with wood pellets and follow the start-up procedure. Preheat the grill, with the lid closed, to 350° F.
4. Arrange the bacon-wrapped hot dogs on the grill grate and cook for 20 to 30 minutes, or until the cheese is melted and the bacon has crisped up. Grill: 350 °F
5. Transfer to the buns and serve immediately with your favorite condiments. Enjoy!

# Delicious Bacon-wrapped Filet Mignon

Servings: 2
Cooking Time: 15 Minutes

**Ingredients:**
- 3 (6 oz) filet mignon steaks
- 1 Teaspoon pepper
- 1 Teaspoon salt
- 2 Clove garlic, minced
- 3 Tablespoon butter, softened
- 3 Slices bacon

**Directions:**
1. Filets don't have much marbling, so when selecting meat look for a rich red color.
2. In a small bowl, combine salt, pepper, garlic and softened butter. Rub on both sides of filet. Let rest 10 minutes.
3. Supply your smoker with wood pellets and follow the start-up procedure. Preheat the grill, with the lid closed, to 450° F.
4. Wrap each steak in a slice of bacon and secure with a toothpick.

5. Place steaks directly on the grill and cook for 5 to 8 minutes on each side, or until the filets reach an internal temperature of 130°F for medium-rare. Enjoy! Grill: 450 °F Probe: 130 °F

# Grilled Rosemary Rack Of Lamb

Servings: 8
Cooking Time: 30 Minutes

**Ingredients:**

➢ 2 Tablespoons Dijon Mustard
➢ 1 Tablespoon Fresh Parsley, Chopped
➢ Chop House Steak Rub
➢ 2 Chine Bones Removed, And Excess Fat Trimmed Racks Of Lamb
➢ 1 Teaspoon Rosemary, Finely Chopped

**Directions:**

1. Place the racks of lamb on a flat work surface, then generously brush the lamb all over with Dijon mustard.

2. Season the meat on all sides with Chophouse Steak seasoning and sprinkle with parsley and rosemary.

3. Supply your smoker with wood pellets and follow the start-up procedure. Preheat the grill, with the lid closed, to 400° F.

4. If you're using a gas or charcoal grill, set it up for high heat.

5. Insert a temperature probe into the thickest part of the rack of lamb and sear the rack, meaty side down for about 6 minutes.

6. Remove the lamb from the grill and turn the temperature down to 300°F.

7. Return the lamb to the grill and lean the two racks against each other so that they stand up, and grill for another 20 minutes, or until the internal temperature reaches 130°F.

8. Remove the racks from the grill and allow to rest for 10 minutes before carving and serving.

# Herb Grilled Venison Stew

Servings: 4 - 6
Cooking Time: 210 Minutes

**Ingredients:**

➢ 2 Bay Leaves
➢ 2 Cups Beef Stock
➢ 3 Carrots, Chopped
➢ 2 Cups Cauliflower Florets
➢ ¼ Tsp Cayenne Pepper
➢ 2 Celery Stalks, Chopped
➢ 4 Garlic Cloves, Minced
➢ 1 Tbsp Italian Parsley
➢ ¼ Tsp Marjoram, Dried
➢ 2 Tbsp Olive Oil
➢ 1 Onion, Chopped
➢ 1 Tsp  Pulled Pork Rub
➢ 1 Cup Red Wine
➢ 1 Tsp Chopped Rosemary, Fresh
➢ (To Taste) Salt And Pepper
➢ 2 Cups Chopped Spinach
➢ 2 Sweet Potatoes, Diced
➢ 2 Tbs Tomato Paste
➢ ½ Cup Tomatoes, Canned And Diced
➢ 2 Lbs. Venison Stew Meat, Cut Into 1" Cubes
➢ 1 Cup Zucchini, Largely Diced

**Directions:**

1. Supply your smoker with wood pellets and follow the start-up procedure. Preheat the grill, with the lid open, to 400° F. If using a gas or charcoal grill, set heat to medium-high heat.

2. Place cast iron Dutch oven directly on grill grates and heat olive oil until shimmering. Add onion, celery, carrot, and garlic and cook, stirring

constantly, for about 5-10 minutes or until onion is translucent.

3. Increase heat on the grill to 500° F. Add venison to the pot and cook until browned on all sides. Add the red wine and allow to simmer for 2 minutes.

4. Add tomato paste, beef stock, mushrooms, sweet potato, tomatoes, rosemary, Pulled Pork Rub, sage, marjoram, cayenne, salt, pepper and bay leaves and mix well to combine. Cover pot, reduce temperature to 300° F and let the stew simmer for at least 2.5 to 3 hours.

5. Remove lid and stir in the cauliflower, spinach, and zucchini. Return cover to pot and simmer an additional 15 minutes. Stir in parsley and serve hot.

## Salt-crusted Prime Rib

Servings: 8
Cooking Time: 180 Minutes

### Ingredients:

➢ 1 1/2 Cup Jacobsen Salt Co. Pure Kosher Sea Salt
➢ 3/4 Cup coarse ground black pepper
➢ 1 Head garlic, peeled
➢ 1/2 Cup rosemary
➢ 2 Tablespoon chile powder
➢ 3/4 Cup extra-virgin olive oil
➢ 1 (15-16 lb) 6-bone prime rib roast

### Directions:

1. In a food processor, combine salt, pepper, garlic cloves, rosemary and chile powder and process until fine. Add the olive oil and pulse to form a paste.

2. Place the prime rib roast on a cutting board, bone-side up and rub with 1 tablespoon of the salt paste.

3. Transfer the meat to a large roasting pan and place bone-side down. Pack the salt paste all over the fatty surface, pressing to help it adhere. Let the prime rib stand at room temperature for 1 hour.

4. Supply your smoker with wood pellets and follow the start-up procedure. Preheat the grill, with the lid closed, to 450° F.

5. Roast the prime rib for 1 hour, or until the crust is slightly darkened. Lower the Traeger temperature to 300°F and roast for about 2 hours and 15 minutes longer, or until an instant-read thermometer inserted into the center of the roast (not touching the bone) registers 125°F for medium-rare. Grill: 450 °F

6. Transfer the roast to a large carving board and let the meat rest for 30 minutes. Grill: 300 °F Probe: 135 °F

7. Carefully lift the salt crust off the meat and transfer to a bowl. Brush away any excess salt.

8. To remove the roast in one piece while keeping the rib rack intact, run a long sharp carving knife along the bones, using them as your guide. Leave on 1/2 inch of meat, or more if reserving for leftovers.

9. Carve the prime rib roast 1/2 inch thick and serve, using some of the crumbled salt crust as a condiment.

## Bbq Beef Ribs

Servings: 4
Cooking Time: 480 Minutes

### Ingredients:

➢ 2 Rack (5-7 lb) 3-bone beef ribs
➢ 3/4 Cup Meat Church Holy Cow BBQ Rub
➢ 2 Cup beef broth, for spritzing

### Directions:

1. Supply your smoker with wood pellets and follow the start-up procedure. Preheat the grill, with the lid closed, to 275° F.

2. Flip the ribs so they are meat side down and remove the membrane off the back of the rack. One trick to do this is to grab the membrane with a paper towel and and pull it off.

3. Apply a heavy coat of Meat Church Holy Cow BBQ Rub on the bone side, thoroughly covering the meat, repeat with second rack. Allow the rub to adhere for 10 minutes. Flip over the rack of ribs and repeat the process.

4. Place the ribs meat side up on the Traeger. You can spritz the ribs every hour or so with a liquid such as beef broth or water to keep them moist.

5. Continue smoking the ribs until probe tender. This is often beyond 210ºF internal temperature. To speed up the process, wrap the ribs after the meat has reached in internal temperature of at least 160ºF. Grill: 275 ˚F Probe: 210 ˚F

6. Remove the ribs from the grill and allow to rest and cool while lightly tented in aluminum foil for 15 to 20 minutes. To serve the ribs whole, make two long cuts or slice the meat off the bone and cube it up for more folks to enjoy.

# Reverse Grilled Potato Bacon Wrapped Steaks

Servings: 2
Cooking Time: 60 Minutes

**Ingredients:**
- 1 Bunch Asparagus
- 4 Bacon, Strip
- BBQ Sauce
- 2 Tbsp Olive Oil
- 1 Bag Potato, Baby

- 2 - 1" Thick Steak, Bone-In Ribeye

**Directions:**

1. Supply your smoker with wood pellets and follow the start-up procedure. Preheat the grill, with the lid open, to 250° F.

2. Wrap two pieces of bacon around each steak. Place on the grates of your preheated Grill. You'll want to cook the steaks until the internal temperature reaches 130°F (for medium-rare). Follow these internal temperatures if you'd like to cook your steak more/less done:

3. Rare: 125°F

4. Medium Rare: 130°F

5. Medium: 140°F

6. Well Done: 160°F

7. If you're cooking your steaks medium rare, it will take around 45 minutes. Put your baby potatoes in a cast iron pan, drizzle with oil and place on grill with the steaks. When your steaks reach the desired internal temperature, remove steaks from the grill and let them rest for 15 minutes. In the meantime, open up your Flame Broiler Plate and crank up the grill to HIGH, keeping your potatoes on the grill. Add the asparagus to the top of the potatoes and cook. When the grill is preheated to HIGH, sear each side of the steak for about 1 minute each. Serve immediately with or without BBQ Sauce.

# Roasted Duck

Servings: 4
Cooking Time: 180 Minutes

**Ingredients:**
- 1 (5-6 lb) duck, defrosted
- Pork & Poultry Rub
- 1 Small onion, peeled and quartered
- 1 orange, quartered

> fresh herbs, such as parsley, sage or rosemary

**Directions:**

1. Remove the giblets and discard or save for another use. Trim any loose skin at the neck and remove excess fat from around the main cavity. Remove the wing tips if desired.

2. Rinse the duck under cold running water, inside and out, and dry with paper towels.

3. Prick the skin all over with the tip of a knife or the tines of a fork; do not pierce the meat. This helps to render the fat and crisp the skin.

4. Season the bird, inside and out, with Traeger Pork and Poultry Rub. Tuck the onion, orange, and fresh herbs into the cavity.

5. Tie the legs together with butcher's string.

6. Supply your smoker with wood pellets and follow the start-up procedure. Preheat the grill, with the lid closed, to 225° F.

7. Place the duck directly on the grill grate. Roast for 2-1/2 to 3 hours, or until the skin is brown and crisp. The internal temperature should register 160°F in the thigh (be sure to avoid the bone as this will give you an inaccurate reading). Grill: 225 °F Probe: 160 °F

8. If the duck is not browned to your liking, increase the grill temperature to 375°F and roast for several minutes at the higher temperature. Grill: 375 °F

9. Tent the duck loosely with foil and allow it to rest for 30 minutes.

10. Remove the butcher's twine and carve. Enjoy!

# Three Ingredient Pot Roast

Servings: 4
Cooking Time: 180 Minutes

**Ingredients:**

> 4 Pound chuck roast, cut into 4 inch chunks

> 2 yellow onions, finely sliced
> 2 Teaspoon kosher salt
> 1/4 Cup extra-virgin olive oil
> freshly ground black pepper

**Directions:**

1. Supply your smoker with wood pellets and follow the start-up procedure. Preheat the grill, with the lid closed, to 400° F.Place half of the chuck roast into a 3-to-4 quart Dutch oven. (Note: if using a roast that is smaller than 4 lbs, make sure to use a smaller Dutch oven as well.) Add half the onions, half the salt, pepper, and half the olive oil. Repeat with the remaining ingredients.

2. Place a tight-fitting lid on the Dutch oven and place on the grill. Cook for 2 to 3 hours, until the chuck roast can be easily shredded with a fork. Reduce the grill temperature to 350°F if the chuck roast is boiling and not simmering. Grill: 400 °F

3. Remove Dutch oven from the grill and remove the lid. Allow the meat to cool, then skim the fat off the top. Alternatively, allow the meat to cool, refrigerate overnight, then skim the fat cap off the meat before reheating the next day. It will keep for 2 days in the fridge.

4. When ready to serve, this pot roast can be topped with many things to make it your own, including my Preserved Lemon Gremolata, chimichurri, peperonata, horseradish cream (horseradish, sour cream and mayo) or a variety of salsas.

# Grilled Dill Pickle Tri Tip Steak

Servings: 4

Cooking Time: 300 Minutes

## Ingredients:

- ➤ BBQ sauce
- ➤ dill pickles
- ➤ jalapeño
- ➤ to taste, java chophouse seasoning
- ➤ 2 tbsp mustard
- ➤ onion, sliced & minced
- ➤ 2 lbs tri tip steak

## Directions:

1. Supply your smoker with wood pellets and follow the start-up procedure. Preheat the grill, with the lid closed, to 225° F. If using a gas or charcoal grill, set it up for low, indirect heat.

2. Rub the mustard all over the tri tip, then season with Java Chophouse.

3. Place the tri tip directly on the grill grates and smoke until the internal temperature reaches 165° F (about 2 1/2 hours).

4. Remove the tri tip from the grill and wrap it in butcher paper. Return the tri tip to the grill and continue to smoke until the internal temperature reaches 200° F (an additional 2 ½ to 3 hours).

5. Remove the tri tip from the grill, and rest for 30 minutes. Slice thin and serve with pickles, jalapeño, onion, and BBQ sauce, if desired.

# COCKTAILS RECIPES

## Smoked Hot Buttered Rum

Servings: 4
Cooking Time: 30 Minutes

**Ingredients:**

➢ 2 Cup water
➢ 1/4 Cup brown sugar
➢ 1/2 Stick butter, melted
➢ 1 Teaspoon ground cinnamon
➢ 1/4 Teaspoon ground nutmeg
➢ ground cloves
➢ salt
➢ 6 Ounce Rum

**Directions:**

1. Supply your smoker with wood pellets and follow the start-up procedure. Preheat the grill, with the lid closed, to 180° F.

2. In a shallow baking dish, combine 2 cups water with all ingredients except for the rum and place directly on the grill grate. Smoke for 30 minutes. Grill: 180 °F

3. Remove from the grill and pour into the pitcher of a blender. Process until somewhat frothy.

4. Pour 1.5 ounces of rum each into 4 glasses. Split hot butter mixture evenly between the four glasses.

5. Garnish with a cinnamon stick and freshly grated nutmeg. Enjoy!

## Smoked Texas Ranch Water

Servings: 4
Cooking Time: 60 Minutes

**Ingredients:**

➢ 3 Whole limes
➢ 1 Tablespoon Blackened Saskatchewan Rub
➢ 12 Ounce blanco tequila
➢ 24 Ounce Topo Chico or other sparkling mineral water
➢ 8 Slices jalapeño, optional

**Directions:**

1. Supply your smoker with wood pellets and follow the start-up procedure. Preheat the grill, with the lid closed, to 225° F.

2. Cut two of the limes in half and sprinkle with Traeger Blackened Saskatchewan Rub. Place the four lime halves on the edge of the grill grate and smoke for 1 hour. Remove from grill and set aside to cool. Grill: 225 °F

3. Pour some of the rub onto a small plate. Cut the third lime into 1/4 wedges and use the lime to rub the rim of 4 cocktail glasses, turn the glasses upside down, and into the rub to salt the rim.

4. Place several ice cubes into your rimmed glasses and pour 3 ounces tequila, 6 ounces Topo Chico, squeeze the juice of one smoked lime (discard after squeezing), and add one fresh lime wedge to each. If using the jalapeño, add one or two slices to each glass (muddle if desired).

5. Stir to combine and enjoy!

## Delicious Smoked Daiquiri

Servings: 2
Cooking Time: 25 Minutes

**Ingredients:**

➢ 2 limes, sliced
➢ 2 Tablespoon granulated sugar
➢ 3 Ounce Rum
➢ 1 Ounce Smoked Simple Syrup

> 1 1/2 Ounce lime juice

**Directions:**

1. Supply your smoker with wood pellets and follow the start-up procedure. Preheat the grill, with the lid closed, to 350° F.

2. Toss the lime slices with granulated sugar and place directly on the grill grate. Cook 20-25 minutes or until grill marks form. Remove from grill and cool. Grill: 350 °F

3. In a mixing glass add rum, Traeger Simple Syrup, and fresh lime juice. Add ice to the mixing glass and shake. Strain contents into a chilled glass.

4. Garnish with a grilled lime wheel. Enjoy!

# Grilled Frozen Strawberry Lemonade

Servings: 4
Cooking Time: 15 Minutes

**Ingredients:**

> 1 Pound fresh strawberries
> 1/2 Cup turbinado sugar
> 8 lemon, halved
> 1/4 Cup Cointreau
> 1/4 Cup simple syrup
> 2 Cup ice
> 1 Cup Titos Vodka

**Directions:**

1. Supply your smoker with wood pellets and follow the start-up procedure. Preheat the grill, with the lid closed, to High heat.

2. Dip the lemon halves in turbinado sugar and place directly on the grill grate. Toss the strawberries with remaining sugar and place next to the lemons.

3. Cook until grill marks develop on both, about 15 min for lemons and 10 min for strawberries.

4. Remove from heat and let cool.

5. Juice grilled lemons straining out any seeds or pulp. Pour into a blender pitcher.

6. Remove stems from grilled strawberries and place in blender pitcher with lemon juice. Add simple syrup, vodka, cointreau, and 2 cups of ice.

7. Puree until smooth and transfer to 4-6 glasses. Garnish with grilled strawberries and grilled lemon slices if desired. Enjoy!

# Smoked Raspberry Bubbler Cocktail

Servings: 2
Cooking Time: 45 Minutes

**Ingredients:**

> 2 Cup fresh raspberries
> Smoked Simple Syrup
> 8 Ounce sparkling wine

**Directions:**

1. Supply your smoker with wood pellets and follow the start-up procedure. Preheat the grill, with the lid closed, to 180° F.

2. Smoked Raspberry Syrup: Place 1 cup fresh raspberries on a grill mat and smoke for 30 minutes. Grill: 180 °F

3. After the raspberries have been smoked, set a few aside for garnish. Place the remainder into a shallow sheet pan with Traeger Smoked Simple Syrup. Place back on the grill grate and let smoke for 45 minutes. Remove from heat and allow to cool. Strain and refrigerate until ready to use. Grill: 180 °F

4. Place 1 ounce of the smoked raspberry syrup in the bottom of a champagne flute and top off with sparkling white wine or champagne.

5. Garnish with smoked raspberries. Enjoy!

# Smoky Scotch & Ginger Cocktail

Servings: 2

Cooking Time: 60 Minutes

**Ingredients:**

- 1 Ounce ginger syrup
- 1/2 Ounce brandied cherry juice
- 1/2 Ounce agave nectar
- 4 Ounce scotch
- 1 1/2 Ounce lemon juice
- 2 Slices grilled lemon, for garnish
- 2 cherry, for garnish

**Directions:**

1. Supply your smoker with wood pellets and follow the start-up procedure. Preheat the grill, with the lid closed, to 180° F.

2. For the smoked ginger cherry syrup: Place ginger syrup, cherry juice and agave nectar in a shallow dish and place the dish directly on the grill grate.

3. Smoke for 60 minutes, or until the mixture has picked up the smoke flavor. Remove from grill and allow to cool for 30 minutes. Grill: 180 °F

4. Place smoked ginger cherry syrup, scotch and lemon juice into a shaker tin and shake with ice. Strain into a glass over fresh ice and garnish with a grilled lemon wheel and cherry. Enjoy!

# Smoked Eggnog

Servings: 4

Cooking Time: 60 Minutes

**Ingredients:**

- 2 Cup whole milk
- 1 Cup heavy cream
- 4 egg yolk
- Cup sugar
- 3 Ounce bourbon
- 1 Teaspoon vanilla extract
- 1 Teaspoon nutmeg
- 4 egg white
- whipped cream

**Directions:**

1. Plan ahead, this recipe requires chill time.

2. Supply your smoker with wood pellets and follow the start-up procedure. Preheat the grill, with the lid closed, to 180° F.

3. Pour the milk and the cream into a baking pan and smoke on the Traeger for 60 minutes. Grill: 180 °F

4. Meanwhile, in the bowl of a stand mixer, beat the egg yolks until they lighten in color. Gradually add 1/3 cup sugar and continue to beat until sugar completely dissolves.

5. After the milk and cream have smoked, add them along with the bourbon, vanilla and nutmeg into the egg mixture and stir to combine.

6. Place the egg whites in the bowl of a stand mixer and beat to soft peaks. When you lift the beaters the whites will make a peak that slightly curls down.

7. With the mixer still running, gradually add 1 tablespoon of sugar and beat until stiff peaks form.

8. Gently fold the egg whites into the cream mixture and then whisk to thoroughly combine.

9. Chill eggnog for a couple hours to let the flavors meld. Garnish with a dash of nutmeg and whipped cream on top. Enjoy!

# Smoke And Bubz Cocktail

Servings: 2

Cooking Time: 45 Minutes

**Ingredients:**

- 16 Ounce POM Juice

- ➤ 2 Cup pomegranate seeds
- ➤ 6 Ounce sparkling white wine
- ➤ 2 lemon twist, for garnish
- ➤ 2 Teaspoon pomegranate seeds

**Directions:**

1. Supply your smoker with wood pellets and follow the start-up procedure. Preheat the grill, with the lid closed, to 180° F.

2. For the Smoked Pomegranate Juice: Pour POM juice and a cup of pomegranate seeds into a shallow sheet pan. Smoke on the Traeger for 45 minutes. Pull off grill, strain, discard seeds and let sit until chilled. Grill: 180 °F

3. Add 1-1/2 ounces of the smoked pomegranate juice to the bottom of a champagne flute.

4. Add sparkling white wine, a few fresh pomegranate seeds and a lemon twist to garnish. Enjoy!

# Smoked Hibiscus Sparkler

Servings: 4
Cooking Time: 30 Minutes

**Ingredients:**

- ➤ 1/2 Cup sugar
- ➤ 2 Tablespoon dried hibiscus flowers
- ➤ 1 Bottle sparkling wine
- ➤ crystallized ginger, for garnish

**Directions:**

1. Supply your smoker with wood pellets and follow the start-up procedure. Preheat the grill, with the lid closed, to 180° F.

2. Place water in a shallow baking dish and place directly on the grill grate. Smoke the water for 30 minutes or until desired smoke flavor is achieved. Grill: 180 °F

3. Pour water into a small saucepan and add sugar and hibiscus flowers. Bring to a simmer over medium heat and cook until sugar is dissolved.

4. Strain out the hibiscus flowers and transfer your simple syrup to a small container and refrigerate until chilled.

5. Pour 1/2 ounce smoked hibiscus simple syrup in the bottom of a champagne glass and top with sparkling wine.

6. Drop in a few pieces of crystallized ginger to garnish. Enjoy!

# Smoking Gun Cocktail

Servings: 2
Cooking Time: 45 Minutes

**Ingredients:**

- ➤ 2 Jar vermouth soaked cocktail onions
- ➤ 3 Ounce vodka
- ➤ 1 Ounce dry vermouth

**Directions:**

1. Supply your smoker with wood pellets and follow the start-up procedure. Preheat the grill, with the lid closed, to 180° F.

2. To make the smoked onion vermouth: Pour jar of vermouth soaked cocktail onions onto a shallow sheet pan. Smoke for 45 minutes. Remove from grill and set aside to chill. Grill: 180 °F

3. To make the cocktail: Add vodka, 1 teaspoon liquid from the smoked onions and dry vermouth to a mixing glass. Shake and strain into a chilled martini glass.

4. Garnish with smoked cocktail onions on a skewer. Enjoy!

# Honey Glazed Grapefruit Shandy Cocktail

Servings: 2
Cooking Time: 20 Minutes

**Ingredients:**

- 4 grapefruits
- 4 Tablespoon honey
- granulated sugar
- 2 Ounce bourbon
- 1 Ounce  Smoked Simple Syrup
- 4 Ounce honey glazed grilled grapefruit, juiced
- 2 Bottle Ballast Point Grapefruit Sculpin

**Directions:**

1.  Supply your smoker with wood pellets and follow the start-up procedure. Preheat the grill, with the lid closed, to 375° F.

2.  For the honey glazed grapefruit: Slice one grapefruit in half and coat with 2 tablespoons honey.

3.  Take the other grapefruit and slice into wheels. Toss the wheels in granulated sugar until well coated.

4.  Place the grapefruit halves and wheels directly on the grill grate, cut side down, and cook for 20 to 30 minutes. Remove from grill and set the wheels aside. Grill: 375 °F

5.  Squeeze the grapefruit halves into a measuring cup. It should yield about 2 oz juice.

6.  Pour the grapefruit juice into a shaker and add bourbon and Traeger Smoked Simple Syrup then top with ice. Shake for 10-15 seconds.

7.  Strain into glass, add ice and fill with beer. Garnish with the grilled grapefruit wheel. Enjoy!

# Ryes And Shine Cocktail

Servings: 2
Cooking Time: 30 Minutes

**Ingredients:**

- 2 lemon, cut into wheels for garnish
- 6 Tablespoon granulated sugar
- 2 Ounce rye
- 1 Ounce bourbon
- 3 Ounce lemon juice
- 1 Ounce  Smoked Simple Syrup
- 6 Dash Fernet-Branca

**Directions:**

1.  Supply your smoker with wood pellets and follow the start-up procedure. Preheat the grill, with the lid closed, to 325° F.

2.  Toss lemon wheels with granulated sugar to coat on both sides. Place wheels directly on the grill grate and cook for 15 minutes on each side or until grill marks form. Grill: 325 °F

3.  Add rye, bourbon, lemon juice, Traeger Smoked Simple Syrup and Fernet-Branca to a shaker and shake until slightly diluted (about 10 to 15 seconds).

4.  Pour into a fresh glass, serve neat and garnish with a grilled lemon wheel. Enjoy!

# Smoked Jacobsen Salt Margarita

Servings: 2
Cooking Time: 1 Day

**Ingredients:**

- kosher sea salt
- 3 Cup Jacobsen Co. Honey
- 6 Ounce tequila
- 4 Ounce fresh squeezed lime juice
- 1/2 Cup Jacobsen Salt Co. Cherrywood Smoked Salt or smoked kosher salt

- ➢ 2 Ounce simple syrup
- ➢ 2 Teaspoon orange liqueur

**Directions:**

1. If making your own smoked salt, take kosher sea salt (however much you want to smoke) and spread it out on a tray.

2. Supply your smoker with wood pellets and follow the start-up procedure. Preheat the grill, with the lid closed, to 165° F.

3. Place tray of salt directly on the grill grate and smoke for about 24 hours, stirring the salt every 8 hours. Once it has smoked for 24 hours, take off grill and use in all your favorite dishes. Note: If you want to skip the long smoke session, use Jacobsen Salt Co. Cherrywood Smoked Salt. Grill: 165 ℉

4. Simple Syrup: Put the honey and 1 cup water in a small saucepan. Cook over low heat, stirring, for about 20 min.

5. Fill a cocktail shaker with ice. Add tequila, lime juice, simple syrup and orange liqueur. Cover and shake until mixed and chilled, about 30 seconds.

6. Place smoked salt on a plate. Press the rim of a chilled rocks glass into the salt to rim the edge. Strain margarita into the glass. Enjoy!

# Smoked Apple Cider

Servings: 2

Cooking Time: 30 Minutes

**Ingredients:**

- ➢ 32 Ounce apple cider
- ➢ 2 cinnamon sticks
- ➢ 4 whole cloves
- ➢ 3 star anise
- ➢ 2 Pieces orange peel
- ➢ 2 Pieces lemon peel

**Directions:**

1. Supply your smoker with wood pellets and follow the start-up procedure. Preheat the grill, with the lid closed, to 225° F.

2. Combine the cider, cinnamon stick, star anise, clove, lemon and orange peel in a shallow baking dish.

3. Place directly on the grill grate and smoke for 30 minutes. Remove from grill, strain and transfer to four mugs. Grill: 225 ℉

4. Finish with a slice of apple and a cinnamon stick to serve. Enjoy!

# Fig Slider Cocktail

Servings: 2

Cooking Time: 15 Minutes

**Ingredients:**

- ➢ 2 peach, halved
- ➢ 4 oranges
- ➢ honey
- ➢ sugar
- ➢ 2 Teaspoon orange fig spread
- ➢ 1 Ounce fresh lemon juice
- ➢ 4 Ounce bourbon
- ➢ 3 Ounce honey glazed grilled orange juice

**Directions:**

1. Supply your smoker with wood pellets and follow the start-up procedure. Preheat the grill, with the lid closed, to 325° F.

2. Pit the peach and cut in half. Cut one of the oranges in half. Glaze the peach and orange cut sides with honey and set directly on the grill grate until the honey caramelizes and fruit has grill marks. Grill: 325 ℉

3. Cut the second orange into wheels and coat with granulated sugar on both sides. Place

directly on the grill grate and cook 15 minutes each side or until grill marks form. Grill: 325 ˚F

4. In a mixing tin, add grilled peaches, bourbon, orange fig spread, fresh lemon juice and honey glazed orange juice.

5. Shake vigorously to blend the juices and fig spread. Strain over clean ice. Garnish with grilled orange wheel. Enjoy!

# Smoked Plum And Thyme Fizz Cocktail

Servings: 2
Cooking Time: 60 Minutes

**Ingredients:**
➢ 6 fresh plums
➢ 4 Fluid Ounce vodka
➢ 1 1/2 Fluid Ounce fresh lemon juice
➢ 2 Ounce smoked plum and thyme simple syrup
➢ 4 Fluid Ounce club soda
➢ 2 Slices smoked plum, for garnish
➢ 2 Sprig fresh thyme, for garnish
➢ 8 Sprig thyme
➢ 2 Cup Smoked Simple Syrup

**Directions:**
1. Supply your smoker with wood pellets and follow the start-up procedure. Preheat the grill, with the lid closed, to 180° F.

2. Cut plums in half and remove the pit. Place the plum halves directly on the grill grate and smoke for 25 minutes. Grill: 180 ˚F

3. For the Plum and Thyme Simple Syrup: After 25 minutes, remove plums from the grill and cut into quarters. Add plums and thyme sprigs to 1 cup of Traeger Smoked Simple Syrup. Smoke the mixture for 45 minutes. Remove from grill, strain and let cool. Grill: 180 ˚F

4. Add vodka, fresh lemon juice and smoked plum and thyme simple syrup to a mixing glass.

5. Add ice and shake. Strain over clean ice, top off with club soda and garnish with a piece of thyme and slice of smoked plum. Enjoy!

# Smoked Berry Cocktail

Servings: 2
Cooking Time: 15 Minutes

**Ingredients:**
➢ 1/2 Cup strawberries, stemmed
➢ 1/2 Cup blackberries
➢ 1/2 Cup blueberries
➢ 8 Ounce bourbon or iced tea
➢ 2 Ounce lime juice
➢ 3 Ounce simple syrup
➢ soda water
➢ fresh mint, for garnish

**Directions:**
1. Supply your smoker with wood pellets and follow the start-up procedure. Preheat the grill, with the lid closed, to 180° F.

2. Wash berries well, spread them on a clean cookie sheet and place on the grill. Smoke berries for 15 minutes. Grill: 180 ˚F

3. Remove berries from grill and transfer to a blender. Puree berries until smooth then pass through a fine mesh strainer to remove seeds.

4. To create a layered cocktail, pour 2 ounces of berry puree in the bottom of a glass. Next, pour 2 ounces of bourbon or iced tea over the back of a spoon into the glass, then 1/2 ounce lime juice and 1/2 ounce simple syrup, top with soda water and ice. Finish with mint or extra berries for garnish.

5. Repeat the same process for 3 more servings. Enjoy!

# Smoked Salted Caramel White Russian

Servings: 4
Cooking Time: 20 Minutes

**Ingredients:**

➢ 16 Ounce half-and-half
➢ salted caramel sauce
➢ 6 Ounce vodka
➢ 6 Ounce Kahlúa

**Directions:**

1. Supply your smoker with wood pellets and follow the start-up procedure. Preheat the grill, with the lid closed, to 180° F.

2. Pour the half-and-half in a shallow baking dish and place directly on the grill grate. In another shallow baking dish, pour 2 to 3 cups of water and place on the grill next to the half-and-half.

3. Smoke both the half-and-half and water for 20 minutes. Remove from the grill and let cool. Grill: 180 °F

4. Place the half-and-half in the fridge until ready to use. Pour the smoked water into ice cube trays and transfer to the freezer until completely frozen.

5. Separate the smoked ice cubes into four glasses. Drizzle the salted caramel sauce around the inside of the glass.

6. Pour 1-1/2 ounce vodka and 1-1/2 ounce Kahlúa into each of the glasses and top with the smoked half-and-half. Enjoy!

## Sunset Margarita

Servings: 2
Cooking Time: 55 Minutes

**Ingredients:**

➢ 4 oranges
➢ 2 Cup plus 1 teaspoon agave
➢ 1/2 Cup water
➢ 1 Ounce burnt orange agave
➢ 3 Ounce reposado tequila
➢ 1 1/2 Ounce fresh squeezed lime juice
➢ Jacobsen Salt Co. Cherrywood Smoked Salt

**Directions:**

1. Supply your smoker with wood pellets and follow the start-up procedure. Preheat the grill, with the lid closed, to 350° F.

2. For the Burnt Orange Agave Syrup: Cut one orange in half and brush cut side with agave. Place cut side down directly on the grill grate and grill for 15 minutes or until grill marks develop. Grill: 350 °F

3. While the orange halves are grilling, slice the other orange and brush both sides of the slices with agave. Place slices directly on the grill grate next to the halves and cook for 15 minutes or until grill marks develop. Grill: 350 °F

4. Remove orange halves from grill grate and let cool. After they have cooled, juice halves and strain. Set aside.

5. Combine 1/4 cup water and agave in a shallow dish and mix well. Remove orange slices from the grill and place in the agave mixture, reserving a few for garnish.

6. Reduce the grill temperature to 180 degrees F and place the shallow dish with agave and oranges directly on the grill grate. Smoke for 40 minutes. Remove from heat and strain. Set aside. Grill: 180 °F

7. To Mix Drink: Rim glass with Jacobsen Smoked Salt. Combine tequila, fresh lime juice, grilled orange juice and burnt orange agave syrup in a glass. Add ice and shake well.

8. Strain into a rimmed glass over clean ice. Garnish with a grilled orange slice. Enjoy!

# Garden Gimlet Cocktail

Servings: 2
Cooking Time: 45 Minutes

**Ingredients:**

- 2 Cup honey
- 4 lemons, zested
- 4 Sprig rosemary, plus more for garnish
- 1/2 Cup water
- 4 Slices cucumber
- 1 1/2 Ounce lime juice
- 3 Ounce vodka

**Directions:**

1. Supply your smoker with wood pellets and follow the start-up procedure. Preheat the grill, with the lid closed, to 180° F.

2. To make smoked lemon and rosemary honey syrup, thin 1 cup honey by adding 1/4 cup water to a shallow pan. Add lemon zest and 2 sprigs rosemary.

3. Place the pan directly on the grill grate and smoke 45 minutes to an hour. Remove from heat, strain and cool. Grill: 180 °F

4. In a cocktail shaker, muddle the cucumbers and 1oz of the smoked lemon and rosemary honey syrup.

5. After muddling, add lime juice, vodka, and ice. Shake and double strain into a coup glass.

6. Garnish with a sprig of rosemary. Enjoy!

# In Delicious Fashion Cocktail

Servings: 2
Cooking Time: 20 Minutes

**Ingredients:**

- 2 Whole orange peel
- 2 Whole lemon peel
- 3 Ounce bourbon

- 1 Ounce Smoked Simple Syrup
- 6 Dash Bitters Lab Charred Cedar & Currant Bitters

**Directions:**

1. Supply your smoker with wood pellets and follow the start-up procedure. Preheat the grill, with the lid closed, to 350° F.

2. Place the lemon and orange peel directly on the grill grate and cook 20 to 25 minutes or until lightly browned. Grill: 350 °F

3. Add bourbon, Traeger Smoked Simple Syrup and bitters to a mixing glass and stir over ice. Stir until glass is chilled and contents are well diluted.

4. Strain into a new glass over fresh ice and garnish with grilled lemon and orange peel. Enjoy!

# Zombie Cocktail Recipe

Servings: 2
Cooking Time: 45 Minutes

**Ingredients:**

- fresh squeezed orange juice
- pineapple juice
- 2 Ounce light rum
- 2 Ounce dark rum
- 2 Ounce lime juice
- 1 Ounce Smoked Simple Syrup
- 6 Ounce smoked orange and pineapple juice
- 2 grilled orange peel, for garnish
- 2 grilled pineapple chunks, for garnish

**Directions:**

1. Supply your smoker with wood pellets and follow the start-up procedure. Preheat the grill, with the lid closed, to 180° F.

2. Smoked Orange and Pineapple Juice: Pour equal parts fresh squeezed orange juice and pineapple juice into a shallow sheet pan and smoke for 45 minutes. Remove and let cool.

Measure out 3 ounces of juice and reserve any remaining juice in the refrigerator for future use. Grill: 180 °F

3. Add dark and light rums, 3 ounces smoked orange and pineapple juice, lime juice and Traeger Smoked Simple Syrup to a mixing glass.

4. Add ice, shake and strain over clean ice into a Tiki glass.

5. Garnish with a grilled orange peel and grilled pineapple. Enjoy!

# Cran-apple Tequila Punch With Smoked Oranges

Servings: 2
Cooking Time: 15 Minutes

### Ingredients:

- ➢ 6 Cup apple juice, chilled
- ➢ 6 Cup light cranberry cocktail
- ➢ 1 Cup cranberries, fresh or thawed
- ➢ 3 Large oranges, halved
- ➢ 1 Cup sugar, for rimming glasses
- ➢ 2 Tablespoon lemon juice
- ➢ 2 Cup reposado tequila
- ➢ 1 Cup orange-flavored liqueur, such as Grand Marnier or Cointreau
- ➢ 2 Bottle sparkling wine (such as prosecco) or sparkling water

### Directions:

1. Combine 1 cup each of the apple and cranberry juices, then pour into ice cube trays. If the cube molds are big enough, place a few cranberries into each cube. Freeze for 6 hours to overnight.

2. Supply your smoker with wood pellets and follow the start-up procedure. Preheat the grill, with the lid closed, to 180° F.

3. Place the orange halves cut-side down on the grill and smoke for 15 minutes. Remove from the grill and juice oranges. Reserve smoked orange juice. Grill: 180 °F

4. When ready to serve, place the sugar on a flat plate. Pour the lemon juice into a bowl that will fit the rim of each glass.

5. Carefully dip the rim of each glass in the lemon juice, then dip in the sugar to create a 1/8" sugar rim. Turn the glass right-side up and allow to dry for a few minutes before using.

6. Just before serving, mix the remaining apple juice, cranberry cocktail and smoked orange juice with the tequila, orange liqueur, and sparkling wine in a large bowl or pitcher. Taste, adding more of any ingredient to meet your preference.

7. When ready to serve, place a few ice cubes in each glass, then pour a cup of the punch over the top. Alternatively, place all of the ice cubes in the punch bowl and allow guests to help themselves. Enjoy!

# Smoked Sangria

Servings: 6
Cooking Time: 45 Minutes

### Ingredients:

- ➢ 1 (750 ml) medium-bodied red wine
- ➢ 1/4 Cup Grand Marnier
- ➢ 1/4 Cup Smoked Simple Syrup
- ➢ 1 Cup fresh cranberries
- ➢ 1 Whole apple, sliced
- ➢ 2 Whole limes, sliced
- ➢ 4 cinnamon stick
- ➢ soda water

### Directions:

1. Supply your smoker with wood pellets and follow the start-up procedure. Preheat the grill, with the lid closed, to 180° F.

2. In a shallow dish, combine red wine, Grand Marnier, Traeger Smoked Simple Syrup and cranberries, and place directly on the grill grate.

3. Smoke for 30 to 45 minutes or until the liquid picks up desired amount of smoke. Remove from grill and place in the fridge to cool. Grill: 180 °F

4. When the mixture has cooled, place in a large pitcher. Add sliced apples, limes, cinnamon sticks and ice to pitcher.

5. Top with soda water, if desired. Enjoy!

## Smoked Pumpkin Spice Latte

Servings: 4
Cooking Time: 45 Minutes

**Ingredients:**
➢ 1 Small sugar pumpkin
➢ olive oil
➢ 1 Can sweetened condensed milk
➢ 1 Cup whole milk
➢ 2 Tablespoon Smoked Simple Syrup
➢ 1 Teaspoon pumpkin pie spice
➢ pinch of salt
➢ cinnamon
➢ whipped cream
➢ shaved nutmeg
➢ 8 Ounce smoked cold brew coffee

**Directions:**
1. Supply your smoker with wood pellets and follow the start-up procedure. Preheat the grill, with the lid closed, to 325° F.

2. Cut the sugar pumpkin in half, scoop out the seeds and discard. Place the pumpkin halves cut side up on a baking sheet and brush lightly with olive oil.

3. Place the sheet tray directly on the grill grate and cook 45 minutes or until the flesh is tender. Remove from heat and place on the counter to cool. Grill: 325 °F

4. When the pumpkin is cool enough to handle, scoop out the flesh and mash until smooth.

5. Place 3 Tbsp of the pumpkin puree in a separate bowl and reserve the remaining for another use.

6. Add the sweetened condensed milk, whole milk, Traeger Smoked Simple Syrup, pumpkin pie seasoning and salt to the pumpkin puree. Whisk to combine.

7. Pour the cold brew over ice, add desired amount of pumpkin spice creamer and top with whipped cream, cinnamon, and shaved nutmeg if desired. Enjoy!

## Delicious Paloma Cocktail

Servings: 2
Cooking Time: 25 Minutes

**Ingredients:**
➢ 4 grapefruit, halved
➢ Smoked Simple Syrup
➢ 10 Stick cinnamon
➢ 3 Ounce reposado tequila
➢ 1 Ounce lime juice
➢ 1 Ounce Smoked Simple Syrup
➢ grilled lime, for garnish
➢ cinnamon stick, for garnish

**Directions:**
1. Supply your smoker with wood pellets and follow the start-up procedure. Preheat the grill, with the lid closed, to 350° F.

2. Grilled Grapefruit Juice: Cut 2 grapefruits in half. Place a cinnamon stick in each grapefruit half and glaze with Traeger Smoked Simple

Syrup. Place on grill grate and cook for 20 minutes or until edges start to burn and it acquires grill marks. Remove from heat and let cool. Grill: 350 °F

3. After grapefruits have cooled, squeeze and strain juice. It should yield 10 to 12 ounces of juice.

4. In a mixing glass, add tequila, lime juice, Traeger Smoked Simple Syrup and 2 ounces of the grilled grapefruit juice.

5. Add ice and shake. Strain over ice in an old fashioned glass.

6. Add a grilled lime slice and cinnamon stick to garnish. Enjoy!

# Batter Up Cocktail

Servings: 2
Cooking Time: 60 Minutes

**Ingredients:**

➢ 2 whole nutmeg
➢ 4 Ounce Michter's Bourbon
➢ 3 Teaspoon pumpkin puree
➢ 1 Ounce  Smoked Simple Syrup
➢ 2 Large egg

**Directions:**

1. Supply your smoker with wood pellets and follow the start-up procedure. Preheat the grill, with the lid closed, to 180° F.

2. Place whole nutmeg on a sheet tray and place in the grill. Smoke 1 hour. Remove from grill and let cool. Grill: 180 °F

3. Add everything to a shaker and shake without ice. Add ice, then shake and strain into a chilled highball glass.

4. Garnish with grated, smoked nutmeg. Enjoy!

# RECIPE INDEX

Donut Bread Pudding 23
Double Chocolate Chip Brownie Pie 22
Double-smoked Cheese Potatoes 66

**E**
Easy Smoked Cornbread 26
Egg Bacon French Toast Panini 59
Egg Sausage Casserole 60
Eyeball Cookies 26

**F**
Fig Slider Cocktail 121
Flank Steak Breakfast Potato Burrito 104
Focaccia 15
Fried Chicken Sliders 83

**G**
Garden Gimlet Cocktail 124
Garlic Bacon Wrapped Shrimp 30
Garlic Blackened Catfish 43
Garlic Pepper Shrimp Pesto Bruschetta 38
Grilled Apple Pie 27
Grilled Artichoke Cheese Salmon 41
Grilled Bacon-wrapped Hot Dogs 110
Grilled Beer Cabbage 65
Grilled Bourbon Pecan Pie 21
Grilled Corn On The Cob With Parmesan And Garlic 63
Grilled Dill Pickle Tri Tip Steak 115
Grilled Double Burgers With Texas Spicy Bbq Sauce 103
Grilled Frozen Strawberry Lemonade 117
Grilled Greek Chicken With Garlic & Lemon 88
Grilled Guacamole 96
Grilled Lemon Lobster Tails 38
Grilled Lemon Salmon 40
Grilled Ratatouille Salad 64
Grilled Rosemary Pork Chops 45
Grilled Rosemary Rack Of Lamb 111

Grilled Salmon Gravlax 32
Grilled St. Louis Style Ribs With Tequila Bbq 49
Grilled Trout With Citrus & Basil 34
Grilled Tuna Steaks With Lemon & Caper Butter 43
Grilled Whole Chicken Stuffed Sausage And Apple 76
Grilled Zucchini Squash Spears 69

**H**
Hawaiian Pineapple Pork Butt 55
Herb Grilled Venison Stew 111
Honey Glazed Grapefruit Shandy Cocktail 120
Hot & Fast Smoked Baby Back Ribs 52
Hot Coffee-rubbed Brisket 101

**I**
In Traeger Fashion Cocktail 124
Injected Drunken Smoked Turkey Legs 84
Italian Herb & Parmesan Scones 22
Italian Meatballs 107

**J**
Jalapeño- & Cheese-stuffed Chicken 80
Jalapeño Beef Jerky 109

**K**
K.i.s.s Texas Bbq Style Brisket 100
Korean Pulled Pork Lettuce Wraps 45

**L**
Leftover Tri Tip Sandwich 107
Lemon Parmesan Chicken Wings 81
Lime Mahi Mahi Fillets 35
Lollipop Drumsticks 85

**M**
Mandarin Chicken Breast 75
Maple-smoked Pork Chops 47
Mashed Red Potatoes 65
Mexican Mahi Mahi With Baja Cabbage Slaw 32

Mustard Garlic Crusted Prime Rib 103

**O**

Old-fashioned Roasted Glazed Ham 46

**P**

Parmesan Roasted Cauliflower 68

Pig Pops (sweet-hot Bacon On A Stick) 91

Pigs In A Blanket 98

Planked Trout With Fennel, Bacon & Orange 44

Portobello Marinated Mushroom 74

Pound Cake 15

Pretzel Bun With Pulled Pork 61

Pretzel Rolls 17

**R**

Reverse Grilled Potato Bacon Wrapped Steaks 113

Roasted Asparagus 72

Roasted Beet & Bacon Salad 72

Roasted Duck 113

Roasted Fall Vegetables 69

Roasted Green Beans With Bacon 70

Roasted Mashed Potatoes 71

Roasted New Potatoes With Compound Butter 73

Roasted Potato Poutine 63

Roasted Pumpkin Seeds 64

Roasted Red Pepper Dip 94

Roasted Sweet Potato Steak Fries 68

Roasted Tomatoes 70

Roasted Vegetable Napoleon 68

Ryes And Shine Cocktail 120

**S**

Salt-crusted Prime Rib 112

Savory Cheesecake With Bourbon Pecan Topping 20

Scalloped Potatoes With Ham, Corn And Bacon 59

Sicilian Stuffed Mushrooms 62

Simple Glazed Salmon Fillets 34

Slow Smoked Rib-eye Roast 102

Smoke And Bubz Cocktail 118

Smoke Roasted Chicken With Herb Butter 82

Smoked Apple Cider 121

Smoked Bacon Brisket Flat 108

Smoked Bbq Ribs 56

Smoked Beet-pickled Eggs 63

Smoked Berry Cocktail 122

Smoked Blackberry Pie 19

Smoked Cashews 90

Smoked Cedar Plank Salmon 33

Smoked Cheesy Alfredo Sauce 21

Smoked Cheesy Chicken Quesadilla 78

Smoked Chicken Fajita Quesadillas 87

Smoked Chicken Leg & Thigh Quarters 88

Smoked Eggnog 118

Smoked Fish Chowder 39

Smoked Garlic Meatloaf 105

Smoked Hibiscus Sparkler 119

Smoked Honey Salmon 41

Smoked Hot Buttered Rum 116

Smoked Jacobsen Salt Margarita 120

Smoked Macaroni Salad 67

Smoked Mashed Potatoes 70

Smoked Peppered Beef Tenderloin 108

Smoked Plum And Thyme Fizz Cocktail 122

Smoked Porchetta With Italian Salsa Verde 54

Smoked Pork Tomato Tamales 47

Smoked Pumpkin Spice Latte 126

Smoked Raspberry Bubbler Cocktail 117

Smoked Salmon Candy 35

Smoked Salted Caramel White Russian 123

Smoked Sangria 125

Smoked Seed Pastrami 105

Smoked Sugar Halibut 33

Printed in the USA
CPSIA information can be obtained
at www.ICGtesting.com
LVHW072006080124
768359LV00008B/898

9 781803 200538